God's Beloved Queer

God's Beloved Queer

Identity, Spirituality, and Practice

ROLF R. NOLASCO JR.

Foreword by Ken Wilson

WIPF & STOCK · Eugene, Oregon

GOD'S BELOVED QUEER
Identity, Spirituality, and Practice

Wipf & Stock
An Imprint of Wipf and Stock Publishers
199 W. 8th Ave., Suite 3
Eugene, OR 97401

www.wipfandstock.com

PAPERBACK ISBN: 978-1-5326-0676-2
HARDCOVER ISBN: 978-1-5326-0678-6
EBOOK ISBN: 978-1-5326-0677-9
Manufactured in the U.S.A.   07/05/19

Interior image: Andrei Rublev's "The Trinity" (Wikimedia Commons PD-Art).

For Salofie Family
especially Ma'Me
I-iddu ku kamu lapa

Contents

Foreword

THIS IS A WORK of searingly insightful psychological, spiritual, theological, and pastoral resistance in memoir form. It is a singular achievement in the growing literature advocating the full inclusion of LGBTQ people—now, at last, emerging from those shaped by (and ultimately rejected by) the evangelical wing of the church.

Oh, how I wish it had been available to me when I was a progressive-leaning evangelical pastor re-thinking the traditional stigmatization of LGBTQ people. What the progressive evangelical pastor lacks—ever wrestling with the "LGBTQ issue," knowing that to cross the line marks the end of evangelical privilege—is a compelling appreciation for the psychological and spiritual suffering of the devout evangelical queer person inflicted by the church. I would surely have moved to full inclusion sooner (and with less self-doubt) had this book been available to me.

With Emily Swan—who married Rachel Murr, having been rejected by her evangelical home church—I now copastor a lovely church honored by the presence of many from the Gender and Sexual Minority community. Only now do I hear the stories and see the effects of religious trauma suffered by queer people. For that reason alone, I am grateful for this book, which will become a tutorial text for me in pastoral ministry. No matter how sympathetic even a progressive evangelical pastor may be, they cannot appreciate the suffering of queer people at the hands of the church. This is only revealed to allies and those who have themselves known what it is like to suffer under the accusation that one's desire for love and companionship is illicit, unholy, perverse, or the new euphemism, "intrinsically disordered."

Dr. Rolf Nolasco writes as a queer person himself. The "we" voice in which he does so—informed by what seems a miraculous reservoir of spiritual resilience—must itself be a source of healing for the queer people who will read this book. But this book is so much more, because Dr. Nolasco is so much more.

He writes from experience as a counselor over many years to LGBTQ people imbedded within an evangelical setting (which for them is a kind of torture chamber.) He writes as a clinician who has done the hard work of integrating attachment theory (and more) into his work. He writes with the gentle voice of a spiritual director, trained to notice and address the movements of the Spirit in a person without defaulting to the off-putting tone of the expert, though expert he is. But above all, he writes as a pastoral theologian. Theology informs the care of souls so it must be pastorally informed, and if it is not, it should be taken with a grain of salt. Nolasco's writing shines in its theological aspect, incorporating the work of Rene Girard—whose scapegoat theory is the most powerful and unifying lens through which to understand the suffering of queer people in the church.

Thanks to Nolasco's integration of Girardian thought, this is so much more than another revisionist look at a handful of clobber texts (he handles those with dispatch early on). This is a deep dive into the gospel itself, as an extension of the project of God with Israel, to unmask the scapegoat mechanism. As a brown person, he is not subject to the white privilege that keeps so many in the American church from seeing the obvious: that the God of Scripture hears the cry and takes the side of the disinherited. To stand with this God is to stand with them.

The effect is breathtaking.

One other thing makes reading this book such a pleasure: unless you are in need of a personality transplant, you will *like* Rolf Nolasco. You will like his voice, his mind, his soul, and his Jesus.

In short, the book in your hands lives up to its powerful title, *God's Beloved Queer.*

Ken Wilson
Ann Arbor Blue Ocean Church

Acknowledgments

QUEERLY BELOVED, THIS LITTLE book would not have been possible without the fierce support, encouragement, and gentle accompaniment of several individuals. First, to my colleagues at Garrett-Evangelical Theological Seminary, especially Lallene Rector, Luis Rivera, and Anne Joh, whose belief in me and in this project widened my theological and pastoral vision for matters queer. Second, to Jordan Bell, Rob MacDonald, Rod Buxton, Kit and Ruth Paraso, and Evan and Julie Sorensen— your friendship over these many years has kept me sane, motivated, and focused especially during moments of intense personal work and dizzying research meandering. Third, to Matthew Wimer, Ian Creeger, and the editorial team at Wipf and Stock, my heartfelt thanks for your guidance, direction, and patience in assisting me to see this project through.

Also, to my mom Lulu Nolasco and sister Lieh Nolasco and the rest of my family in Winnipeg, Manitoba, Canada, thank you for just letting me do my work over Christmas break while you all got busy to ensure that I was fed, rested, and refreshed. I am who I am today because of you all.

Lastly, the impetus for this project is borne out of my queer siblings who have shown great resilience in the midst of rejection, unwavering faith even in moments of doubt, and love in the face of hate and exclusion. You all are my heroes and inspiration. To the late René Girard and to James Alison, my conversation partners, thank you for opening up a new of way of living, loving, and desiring.

In Christi Gloriam!

Introduction

Yes, you are loved as you are!
And your love is as pure and genuine and true as the love of another!
So, let us celebrate this love
Love that mirrors the consummate love of Christ
A victimless, gratuitous, and creative love
That declares with such delightful cheer that
You are, without a doubt
God's Beloved Queer!

I WANT TO START our journey together with this bold claim, perhaps, to set the stage of what is to come in the pages following. Love is the beginning point of this journey. It is also the destination I would like to end up in. It is not "Love Wins," per se, as that phrase seems to signal that there are winners and losers in the "game of love." And for most of us, there is enough pain to speak of since we have been barred from or are always on the losing end of this game as our love is considered defective, distasteful, and an aberration of the "right kind of love." "Love Perseveres" is more apt, it seems, because in the face of all that there is still that part, albeit small or obscure, that remained steadfast to this love. Hidden or flickering and even dangerous as this may feel at times, our desire to love cannot be maimed because we are created in love, for love, and to love by God, whose affections towards us defies human logic, categories, expectations. God is Love, and you and I are part of this ever-expanding love that seeks to flourish us all in all ways possible.

We begin this journey by taking on a road less travelled. It starts not with a vigorous argument for acceptance that is backed by careful exegetical work, but a gentle whisper of invitation to reframe our status as God's Beloved. From there, we will explore the inner psychological and spiritual landscape of queer Christians from myriad angles, giving primacy to our lived experience and backed by explanatory models. In a way, it is a form of exegesis, if you come to think of it—a hermeneutic of a living human document, of a particular queer experience. Hence, I make no universal claims in my interpretive moves, and if I have veered towards that, I covet your empathy and compassion. I am acutely aware of how varied the queer experience is and that I am only peering into a variation of it, albeit from a uniquely personal, professional, social, and religious matrix that has been home for me all these many years. I hope, though, that as you peruse these pages, you will find something that echoes within, something that you can take as bread for your own journey towards self-discovery, acceptance, and celebration in whatever stage of (queer) life you may be. Remember, God loves you as you are wherever you are. And there is more in that inexhaustible love that is spilling over to reach the very depths of our being no matter the plan to contain, ration, and dispense it conditionally.

For many gay Christians, discovering that our erotic desires are oriented differently, not deficiently, can cause so much confusion, shame, and fear, especially when seen through the lens of conservative and traditional teachings on human sexuality. The blast of uncompromising oppressive discourse on homosexuality renders our humanity—our thoughts, feelings, desires, and longings, not just about our sexuality, but everything that constitutes our personhood—suspect, defective, and unacceptable. Inevitably, these teachings, which have also been accorded a divine status, laid doubt on the authenticity and veracity of our inmost desires to love, know, and serve God. In other words, they have created a dissonance, a widening chasm between our bodily integrity and our deepest yearnings for the spiritual. Being gay is contradictory to being Christian sums up the core of its teachings. And the only acceptable expression of human sexuality is heterosexuality, and the only acceptable expression of human love is heterosexual love. So, better "man up and straighten up" (pun intended) if you want to be considered one of us—is the enforced edict that when obeyed grants inclusion into the "people of God."

The aftereffect of these encounters is heart-wrenching, as we are often left only with their scathing words that haunt and taunt us for no end. The repetitive nature of this discourse that is suffused with familiar biblical jus-tifications and then couched in strong emotional negative valence creates an impression deep into the structure of our brain that then provokes a ripple effect which impacts our psychological and spiritual lives. Fraught by conflicting emotions and often disparaging self-talk, we end up retreat-ing further into circuitous self-condemnatory habits often hidden from the glare of others. In our quest for acceptance and belongingness, psychologi-cal needs intrinsic to being human, we have learned to project a persona that is not ours, but a caricature of other people's patterns of desires. Given our immersion in oppressive religious structures and relationships that are based on conditions of worth, it is often difficult to imagine that things could be different. The result, tragically, is often dim. The constant prick of estrangement piercing through the very depths of our being creates a gap-ing wound that takes us to a place of agony which makes us groan earnestly and pray aimlessly, often in silence and isolation. Where does my help come from? A cry of desperation? Perhaps! But it could also be a flicker of hope that can never be extinguished because it points to a reality far greater and more spacious and creative than what has been given to us by the larger social world.

And so, in the midst of this perilous and incredibly solitary journey, we will fan into flame this profound longing to be relieved from this in-duced splintering of our basic humanity. We will keep alive the hope that we are being ushered into an entirely new experience, of being embraced lovingly and unreservedly by God, who takes delight and liking in us just as we are. That glimmer of hope will never go on unnoticed. God in Jesus Christ shatters these false gods that revel around exclusion and transcends human categories and requirements for inclusion in the unfolding of this new creation. On the cross with his outstretched arms, he bids us to come to receive our inheritance as heirs of God, and the empty tomb is a marker of what is yet to come for us, our own flourishing, starting from where we are. The configuration of our flourishing, though varied, will bear fruits of personal (e.g., emotional stability and resilience, vitality, engagement, posi-tive relationships) and political significance (e.g., working towards social justice, racial and gender equality for all), and is ultimately the manifest work of the Triune God in us. More will be said about this later on. For now, it is best to frame our conversation with the knowledge that this gratuitous display of love is a testament to the true heart of God—God is for us and is over against nothing or no one, at all!

God is more like nothing at all than like anything that is, because God is not a member of the same universe as anything that is, not in rivalry with anything that is. God is not an object within our ken; we find ourselves as objects within God's ken. God is massively prior to us, and God's protagonism is hugely more powerful than any possible action or reaction which we might imagine.[1]

Hence, we are not a threat to God. God has no part in the machinery of exclusion and religious violence that often characterizes discourse on homosexuality and dealings with gay Christians. I know, this is a lot to take in. It may even sound strange at first, as we are not used to hearing God described to us this way. I hope, though, that in my own little way through these pages I can share a bit of that truth. Only one thing I ask of you: take this initial courageous step of faith with me, and with the grace of God let us reimagine ourselves being in the inside of God, being the object of God's ken, and whisper this sweet prayer to each other, as we embark on this journey together.

I desire for you to realize what the Father [sic] has always envisaged for you, so that you may know the magnitude of his intent and be dynamically reinforced in your inner being by the Spirit of God. This will ignite your faith to fully grasp the reality of the indwelling Christ. You are rooted and founded in love. Love is your invisible inner source, just like the root system of a tree and the foundation of a building. The dimensions of your inner person exceed any other capacity that could possibly define you. Love is your reservoir of super human strength which causes you to see everyone equally sanctified in the context of the limitless extent of love's breath and length and the extremities of its dimensions in depth and height. I desire for you to become intimately acquainted with the love of Christ on the deeper possible level; far beyond the reach of a mere academic, intellectual grasp. Within the scope of this equation God finds the ultimate expression of himself [sic] in you. So that you may be filled with all the fullness of God! Awaken to the consciousness of his closeness! Separation is an illusion! Oneness was God's idea all along! He desires to express himself through your touch, your voice, your presence; he is so happy to dwell in you! There is no place in the universe where he would rather be! We celebrate him who supercharges us powerfully from

---

1. Alison, *Broken Hearts and New Creations*, 269.

within. Our biggest request or most amazing dream cannot match the extravagant proportion of his thoughts towards us.[2]

A BRIEF EXCURSUS

Before continuing on, let me take a short excurses to discuss, at the outset, the challenges inherent in any discussion on sexual identity, especially when seen through the lens of the Western contemporary Christian context. This book, like those that offer a reflection on the gay issue, is already implicated in some sort of binary thinking that has become so intertwined with the discourse. In fact, if we follow the debate, we discover that often such fixed and binary positions—homosexuality versus heterosexuality; affirming versus negating the morality of same-sex desires and related issues such as ordination and marriage—tend to obscure or trivialize the complexity of the issue and derails or prohibits any possibility for a radically meaningful and respectful dialogue. It also feels "virtually impossible to find fresh ways to move forward when our imaginations are bound by the culture that shaped them."[3] To this I add the limiting of religious imagination, as well especially when discourse on human sexuality is organized by a singular way of reading and interpreting the Scriptures. It is my intention to try to subvert this polarity by turning the discourse on its head, and I hope that this book contributes to a different kind of conversation that expands our religious and ethical horizons.

The emergence and influence of social constructionism on our understanding of human sexuality has valuable insights to offer in this conversation. These theories proffer the notion that categories such as sexuality or gender are external to the individual, defined by social understandings and discourse,[4] and make explicit our contingency on language given to us by the social other by which to interpret human experience.[5] These constructions are usually defined by the dominant group to reinforce social hierarchy and privileges and are "bound up with the question of power and with the problem of who qualifies as the recognizably human and who

---

2. Eph 3:16–20, *The Mirror Bible*.

3. Paris, *End of Sexual Identity*, 27.

4. DeLamater, "Essentialism vs. Social Constructionism," 10–13.

5. DeLamater, "Essentialism vs. Social Constructionism," 10–13.

does not."[6] Though I give more credence to the complex interplay between biology and environment, I find their insights compelling especially when it comes to the importance of human agency in challenging the pattern of desires or constructions instituted by the social other since it is from within this domain where resistance of all sorts against all types of violence can be found. Part of the effort of resisting the dominant discourse is to find an alternative way of naming and interpreting reality that includes all, and not just the few.

Speaking of language, let me also assert that the word "homosexual," which I use heuristically in this text, is not merely a benign descriptor anymore. The term carries with it so much (dead) weight and has been co-opted as a device for separation, exclusion, cruelty, and violence. As a form of resistance, several authors have problematized the term by tracing when it first appeared in contemporary English versions of the Bible and what the surrounding circumstances were that turned a description to an ammunition. In fact, it was discovered that it was only in the 1946 New Testament Revised Standard Edition where the word "homosexual" first appeared, and its intent was more ideological and cultural than theological.[7] In the same vein, others have offered alternative readings of "clobber texts" that take seriously the context in which these texts were written or composed. Take, for example, the word "homosexual" in 1 Corinthians 6:9. According to scholars, this term "does not mean "homosexual" in the modern sense of a person of a specific erotic disposition for the simple reason that the ancient world possessed no comparable concept of a specifically homoerotic sexual identity . . . that in the first century the most common and readily available form of male homoerotic sexual activity was a master's or patron's exploitation of young male slaves."[8] In other words, these texts have to do more with power and privilege that are often concealed in order to maintain the established social order. These are linguistic or semantic issues that get downplayed to support a singular reading of these texts which often produce spiritual and psychic damage in its wake.

All these challenges can be framed as the outcome of our attachment to the sexual identity framework, a decidedly Western nineteenth-century construct "grounded in the belief that the direction of one's sexual desire is

6. Butler, *Undoing Gender*, 2.

7. Baldock, *Walking the Bridgeless Canyon*; see also Boswell, *Christianity, Social Tolerance*; Kuefler, *Boswell Thesis*.

8. Hart, *New Testament*; see also Halperin, *One Hundred Years*.

identity-constituting,"[9] that we are whom we are attracted to—worse, that that is all there is about us. Undeniably, our obsession to this framework betrays to a great extent the prismatic and layered dimensions of what it means to be human. It has also majorly contributed to so much oppression, discrimination, and injustice towards those considered to be in the sexual minority group because this framework "keeps us rooting after moral law and clinging to moral judgment"[10] that is often rigid, one-sided, and otherizing.

How? Well, the moral logic attached to the sexual identity framework often divides people into two groups with distinguishable codes and ethics—the in-group, or those who adhere to its moral codes, and the out-group, or outsiders who are seen as a threat because of their differing beliefs that challenge the established norm and values of the in-group.[11] The otherization of the out-group, as the normative discourse on homosexuality shows, is infused by an overestimation of the in-group and the degradation of their counterpart. Their apparent "alternative life choices" are considered to be a reflection of their flawed nature, their character or essence.[12] Consequently, a clear demarcation is drawn by emphasizing their difference from the in-group, "pushing the unpleasantness away to a more comfortable psychological distance and pushing the persons away with it . . . purely because we have beliefs about other people which lead us to push them into hated out-groups."[13] In other words, contact with the out-group is seen as a huge threat, which is often reinforced or legitimized by an attribution of disgust and made even before any encounter has taken place.[14] Much of the debate, then and now, regarding the full inclusion of the queer community into the religious life of faith communities reflects this social dynamic and centers around the so-called "essence trap"[15] strongly reinforced by personal and "cultural politics of emotions."[16]

9. Paris, *End of Sexual Identity*, 41.

10. Paris, *End of Sexual Identity*, 78.

11. Taylor, *Cruelty*, 8.

12. Taylor, *Cruelty*, 9.

13. Taylor, *Cruelty*, 9.

14. Ahmed, *Cultural Politics of Emotions*, 87.

15. Ahmed, *Cultural Politics of Emotions*, 87.

16. Ahmed, *Cultural Politics of Emotions*, 9.

THE LANDSCAPE

This book recenters the conversation back to what I believe constitutes our true identity. That is, we all are beloved children of God whose image and likeness we bear—we are God's Beloved Queers. As the title of this book glaringly and boldly declares, the position I take in matters gay is affirmative, especially in terms of our personhood and the shape of flourishing that this status or identity will bring to fruition. I have drawn from a wide range of disciplines—from pastoral theology, spirituality, counseling psychology, affective neuroscience, anthropology—and other cognate disciplines so as to offer us a more nuanced description of what it means to be beloved queers of God, particularly the terrain of our inner psychological and spiritual queer lives, along with practices that will help support our flourishing. I have also included stories of personal nature, mine and those of others, to help "flesh out" ideas I want to share with you.

Chapter 1 revolves around the queering of our identity, of going deeper into layers upon layers of forced descriptions imposed from outside that often get internalized as our own so we can discover and get reacquainted with and slowly embrace anew our identity as beloved. In a way, this chapter is sort of a manifesto of our status as God's Beloved Queers created in the image and likeness of God. We are therefore icons of the Triune God just like everyone else, a window into the spacious, gratuitous, and transforming love of God. This chapter parses the title of the book into two—Queer and God's Beloved—to highlight the theological method that underlies the re-casting of our identity as well as the outcome of this interpretive move to substantiate the claim.

Chapter 2 tackles our inner psychological life and needs such as attachment and relatedness, orientation and control, self-esteem enhancement and pleasure maximization that are basic to all human beings yet are sources of deprivation for many gay Christians. This is one aspect of the queer life that gets lost in the conversation, almost seen as immaterial or irrelevant to many, that we are somehow undeserving to have these basic human needs fulfilled. Sadly (and this we have witnessed constantly), repeated and ongoing frustrations or violations of these needs result in impairments in psychological functioning, compromised health, and diminished quality of life. These are realities that most individuals in our community struggle with, and I hope that by making this explicit we can have better understanding of our interior life, make no apologies for our efforts to meet these needs, and begin to chart a path for our flourishing.

Chapter 3 delves into the psychological and socio-cultural and religious dynamics of scapegoating by which gay Christians are subjected to relentlessly. It also unpacks the deep-seated cognitive, behavioral, and emotional brain mechanisms that get implicated or activated in this social mechanism of exclusion. As numerous scientific studies have shown, constant exposure to messages of hate and fear hijacks the brain by turning off its empathy and compassion brain circuitry and puts it on high alert, always ready to deeply defend held but often unexamined belief systems. Alarmingly, the shaping power of these types of experiences on a malleable and plastic brain is often undetected and unrecognized, and therefore vulnerable to being usurped for destructive purposes, either to oneself and/or others. Through the lens of mimetic theory, this section also exposes the co-opting of the sacred to legitimize this victimizing mechanism by giving it the divine stamp of approval, and to show how such pernicious tactic secures a sense of peace, order, and unanimity for many. But there is a ray of hope, and that hope is the undoing of this sacred violence by Jesus Christ, who occupied the place of shame on the cross to set us free and to usher in a new and radical way of doing life together.

Chapter 4 is the centerpiece of the book, and the underlying premise here is that God has got nothing to do with the mechanism of exclusion and has come to us to subvert any notion of order, goodness, and moral understanding through the example of Christ, our model and mediator of God's own victimless and consummate love. This chapter offers a queer reading of atonement theory and presents a more compelling portrait of what Christ has accomplished for us on the cross. It then proceeds into an exploration of what this new way of being looks like for us, what it means to imitate Christ, and how the practice of contemplation, participation in eucharistic life, and compassion might help us in this lifelong journey towards becoming like him. Our identity and status as God's Beloved enjoin us, as our first response, to imitate the kenotic or self-giving love of Jesus Christ in the concreteness of our queer lives.

Chapter 5 is where the rubber meets the road, so to speak. The thrust of this chapter is to offer concrete spiritual and psychological practices using the mnemonic "BELOVED" that I hope will help nourish and cultivate our inner being as we progress in this journey towards acceptance, celebration, and communion with others and God. Such soul habits are our way of embodying a dynamic and inspired faith that bears the fruit of diffusive and forgiving love without limits and that transcends resentment, protest, or revenge. This is not an act of heroic self-sacrifice, but as a flowering of a newly formed identity as God's Beloved Queers whose lives are hidden in Christ and are called to become cofacilitators in the flourishing of all human beings in all its manifold expressions. Embracing this new identity comes out of a deeply felt sense or intimate knowing of being loved unconditionally and "being-held-in being over against nothing at all . . . by a force of invisible gratuity depending on nothing at all, part of no argument, simply giving life out of nothing."[17]

In a way, what I am trying to accomplish in this little book is to make familiar strange and the strange familiar. For most of us who had grew up and had immersed in the traditional or more conservative evangelical strand of Protestant Christianity, our status in the whole economy of God is that of an outsider looking in. It is a familiar space that I am now making strange by claiming that we, too, are jars of clay and vessels of the new creation that make manifest the glory of Christ (2 Cor 4:4–7), just like everyone else. Since we are recipients of God's manifold works and have been delightfully declared as God's Beloved, we have this amazing opportunity to be cocreators with God in the renewal and restoration of creation. The only way to make that happen is to go back to the heart of our faith, that is, to imitate the example of Christ. This is a strange admonition that is now made familiar by encouraging us to take the lead in creating spaces of consummate and forgiving love as a way of drawing others to Christ, no matter the cost. This way, we gradually dismantle the divide that separates us all, and we work towards communion that does not operate on the mechanism of exclusion.

SOJOURNERS TOGETHER

I suspect that this book will evoke feelings of curiosity and familiarity or discomfort and bewilderment. Others might even find it offensive, even sacrilegious, and I take no offense in that. To a certain degree, I know and understand where these responses might be coming from and I am in no position to pass judgments. What I hope I have been able to do here, though, is to foster an attitude of spaciousness and hospitality that can hold together differing voices while championing the immense value of each person regardless of where we are at in the conversation.

17. Alison, *Faith Beyond Resentment*, 10.

There are several groups of people I have in mind, fellow sojourners I call them, and pray that this book will find its way to them. The book is written for gay Christians who still have this lingering sense of their sacred worth and have held onto their faith without fail, regardless of how they have been treated or what others have said about them because of their sexuality. I would like to encourage you to stay on course, to keep the faith, and I hope that this book will help amplify that which you know intimately and intuitively to be your birthright—that you are God's Beloved. It is also my desire that through these pages you will learn more about your interior psychological life, the effects of scapegoating, and the spiritual treasures you have been gifted with so you can begin to reenvision your life that aligns more with who you are and who you are becoming as God sees you, not in rivalry with you but in concert with you. Remember, there is no other place God would rather be than in you, in the immediacy and embodied reality of your life. This is exactly where God will also begin the work of flourishing you and discerning what this looks like may be nerve-racking at first, but I can assure you it is worth discovering and pursuing.

For my brothers and sisters in the Lord who have been "out and proud" for quite a while now, this is for you as well. I commend you for your courage in stepping out and claiming your place in the kin-dom of God in the face of opposition and oppression. In the midst of this, perhaps, there is still some residual resentment, guilt, or even shame that nags at you from time to time. If so, I hope that you will gain something of value, a sort of guidance or direction, a reframing of your experience, a spiritual practice that will help supplement the internal psychological and spiritual work that you have been doing to address these still-to-be-processed issues. You may even find something of practical benefit as you continue to accompany those who are still struggling with finding integration, alignment, and coherence with their lived experience and the life of faith.

As well, there are many other travelers who have been our fierce advocates in this journey. Allies, we call them, and we give them a shoutout for being our shield when everything seems to be crumbling down around us. May you find in these pages a sense of renewed commitment, not only in helping us remember the true source of our identity, but also in partnering with us in our quest to become one of the answers to Jesus' priestly prayer—that all of them may be one, Father, just as you are in me and I am in you. May they also be in us so that the world may believe that you have sent me (John 14:21)—not in striving towards uniformity in belief, but in our shared calling to be in union with Christ, who then makes us one.

Many still will find the content of this book problematic—theologically or otherwise. We all approach this subject matter from many different vantage points as a result of being given to a particular social order, inherited belief system and practices, that is prior to all of us. This pre-packaged discourse has become so intertwined with our personal, social, and spiritual life that it is often overwhelmingly difficult, even threatening to entertain alternative explanations. Often these differences are so stark it feels as though there is such a divide that seems impossible for us to bridge. Numerous times, though, I have been on the receiving end of someone else's grace despite our divergent views, and it is my desire to exhibit the same level of empathy in situations where it is needed the most. On that note, I hope that you will find it within yourself to suspend some reservations about the book and give it a try. If nothing comes out of it, then let me extend my gratitude for allowing our story a space in your heart.

In the end, regardless of where we land after this journey together, let us discern together and inhabit the space that God is opening up for all of us, a space that includes us all and leads us to the fullness of life. This generous and gratuitous spaciousness towards which God is leading us is made possible by the ongoing and dynamic presence of the crucified and risen Christ through the Holy Spirit who makes everything new, and is releasing us to a new way of being together where our sacred worth is acknowledged and prized, and differing voices are held in humility so that we can expand our circle of inclusion rather than erect barriers of exclusion.

CHAPTER ONE

Queering Identity

GOD'S BELOVED QUEER ARE three words you don't normally string together, let alone use as a self-descriptor. In fact, using this identifier is considered sacrilegious, especially in conservative contexts that hold and affirm a negative view towards homosexuality with such sweeping certitude. Even some gay Christians will struggle with this ascription because of an internalized belief that renders their personhood, not just their sexuality, as an affront to God and a clear infraction of Christian witness. For them, the phrase "God's Beloved" is an epithet that can easily be imputed upon and embraced by anyone and everyone in the Christian fold except, of course, if you are gay. It is considered an oxymoron, because being Christian and gay are two worlds apart. They simply do not fit.

Well, even though many a Christian believes this to be true, it does not have to be our truth. The bestowed identity as God's Beloved can be ours, too. However faint or shaky our claim to this might be, God's love and affirmation of our humanity remains steadfast no matter how much others try to limit and constrain the nature and expression of that great love. It will not be easy, of course, to fan into flame this flickering light symbolizing our deepest longing for love and acceptance as forces both inside and outside seem so ferocious and relentless to snuff it out. But the source of fire that will keep this light aflame is undeterred by the howling of judgment, condemnation, and misrepresentations heaped upon us, and instead reminds us that nothing, no thing, and no one, even ourselves, can separate us from the love of God in Christ (Rom 8:35), ever. We are, after all, God's Beloved Queers, created in the image of God (Gen 1:27), and therefore are sacred icons of the Triune God just like everyone else, a window into the spacious, gratuitous, and transforming love of God. When we let this fiery love consume us, it will set our heart ablaze, refining us so that all doubts, self-condemnation, prickly and piercing judgments, and impurities will begin to melt away to reveal our truest nature—precious in the sight of God, just like gold and silver (Mal 3:2). In this context, we truly are flaming queers.

Before we go any further, I would like to delineate the words—God's Beloved Queer—that are joined together to form what I so boldly call our inviolable identity and a term of endearment. At its core, this designation signifies deep affection and delight of the Lover towards the Beloved and signals the possibility for deep intimacy, a flourishing of our humanity, and unbreakable communion and union with the divine. As well, the ensuing exploration will serve as a theological framework, albeit experimental and provisional, that underpins my own understanding of what it means to be God's Beloved Queer.

ISN'T IT QUEER?

Let us start with the word "queer," a term that was once derogatory but is now used as a marker for transgressive acts, a subversion against the dominant discourse around issues of human identity and human sexuality.[1] This book itself is queer in its attempt to position gay Christians as worthy recipients of God's Love, who deeply desires and participates with us in our flourishing with all the gifts and graces we have been blessed with, starting from where we are in the present moment and into an open future that awaits us.

Here we are the central characters like everyone else, not peripheral or marginal, on the inside of God's creative wisdom, called to partake in revealing the presence of God in everything.[2] We who have been seen as a distortion of God's "ideal" is now catapulted to a place of honor, as am-

---

1. Foucault, *History of Sexuality*; see also Bakshi, *Decolonizing Sexualities*; Butler, *Gender Trouble*; Cheng, *Radical Love*; Comstock and Henking, *Queerying Religion*; Loughlin, *Queer Theology*; Sedgwick, *Epistemology of the Closet*; Sullivan, *Critical Introduction to Queer Theory*; Talvacchia, *Queer Christianities*.

2. See WCCM, "One in Christ."

bassadors for Christ (2 Cor 5:20) mediating *Immanuel*—God with us—in and through our queer lives. Now that is truly a subversive act, a queer reimagining of God's design for our lives, a reframing of our ultimate status that is on equal footing with all of our brothers and sisters in the household of faith.

In an unapologetically seditious manner, we could also say that we are engaged in queer theologizing, in which speech about God comes from a place that has long been silenced or shunned by conventions or traditions. We endeavor to queer theology by interrogating deeply defended theological beliefs, assumptions, and expectations around issues of sexuality deemed as gospel truths and to make theology queer by creating spaces where our voices, stories, and theologizing are acknowledged and affirmed as a legitimate source of speaking about and reflecting on divine matters.[3]

And in giving voice to our experience and laying claim our unique contribution to the manifold work, word, and will of God here on earth, we come as a queer collective—lesbian, gay, bisexual, transgender, questioning, intersex, asexual and our allies (LGBTQIA+)—who stand in solidarity, one with the other, in pursuit of a world where justice, peace, and mercy reign not just for our community, but for all people. In this context, the word "queer" is used as a noun and is an apt redescription of who we are as individuals and as a community with a shared commitment to break the chains of injustice of all kinds. We are still quite distant from making this a lived reality. And often the burden is too heavy to carry. But we are not alone, nor are we supposed to carry it all by ourselves. Justice-making is ultimately generated, inspired, and sustained by the transforming power of the Spirit of God (Luke 4:18–19) in us who is refashioning a different kind of human community of which we play a significant part. From the queer eye, this new way of conducting our life together involves a critique or deconstruction of the binary and often oppositional constructs regarding sexuality (homosexuality vs. heterosexuality) and gender identity (male vs. female) so entrenched in human systems and institutions and a creative reconstruction of a different way of speaking about and relating to one another.

As part of this hermeneutical process, we will go back to a rereading of the so-called "clobber text" (Gen 1:27; 19; Lev 18:22; 20:13; Deut 23:17–18; Rom 1:26–27; 1 Cor 6:9; 1 Tim 1:10) that will hopefully breathe new vitality into an otherwise life-negating interpretation we are accustomed to hear. I

---

3. Halperin, "Normalization of Queer Theory," 2–47.

must alert you, though what is proffered here is in a condensed abridged form, since the pivot on which this book hangs is based not on these passages, but on Jesus Christ as the key and living hermeneutical principle: "the one who opens, and points towards, and is himself, that Presence."[4] In this dynamic process, we assume the posture of the disciples on the road to Emmaus (Luke 24) who attentively listen to Christ, who in turn interprets the Scripture and in so doing "[makes] it possible for the hearers to reconstruct their own imagination, and duly fired up, go out to reconstruct the world."[5] In other words, we let Christ, through his Spirit, break through these texts, break through our hearts and mind, and we allow him to read us and direct our way of reading and seeing other living and equally favored human documents.

But just to satisfy a bit of your curiosity—and this may not come as a surprise to you—these awfully contested texts are deeply embedded in a particular sociocultural context, and therefore has a worldview and social order unique and particular to that time. Upon closer examination by queer theorists and theologians, these singly interpreted passages that constitute the corpus of discourses on human sexuality betray a hidden and insidious mechanism of control, domination, and subjugation that purports to safeguard the normative status of heterosexual males over against their variants. These seditious readings give credence to the constructed nature of sexuality that has social, historical, cultural, and political origins instead of a fixed and factual human feature.[6] This is not to say that these texts are bereft of anything good to say. However, as will be established later on, definitive theological assertions or moral claims regarding homosexuality, at least as we understand this term in our contemporary context, cannot be found from these texts.

On that note, let me draw the curtain just enough to reveal some of the inner yet complex physiological and psychological dynamics of being gay, albeit personal and subjective. When the subject of homosexuality arises, the focus tends to be solely placed on homosexual practices, as if that is the only thing we care about all the time. In these conversations, the genital takes precedence over the personal. The tone becomes utterly intrusive and quite voyeuristic, and evokes all sorts of judgments which, in

---

4. Alison, *Faith Beyond Resentment*, 42.
5. Alison, *Faith Beyond Resentment*, 42.
6. Spargo, *Foucault and Queer Theory*, 17.

the process, obscures the person who feels in a deeply profound way these human desires.

As a descriptive device (and risking the possibility of getting roped into some sort of binary thinking), the word "homosexuality," which was only used as a sexual and social category in the 1870s,[7] could mean very similar to sexuality in that it has to do with our sexual feelings and desires, the kind of person we are attracted to, and the various sexual activities in which we want to participate.[8] In other words, it encompasses dimensions of our psychological or mental life, relational preferences, and bodily needs and desires woven together to make us feel (or do) a certain way towards a particular person. For those of us who self-identify as queers, this object of erotic desire, attraction, and affection is directed towards someone of the same sex.

As a teenager, I remember getting all giddy and flustered every time I laid eyes on a schoolmate. A sudden burst of excitement would come flooding in at the mere thought of spending a good chunk of time near him. Should I sit next to him or inconspicuously watch him from afar? Must I display my acquired knowledge and preference for the social sciences to draw his attention, or remain disinterested so as not to intimidate him? Might I appear nonchalant when I get invited to do things, or express delight to keep him company? These conflicted thoughts and feelings and subsequent bodily enactments betray a state of mind that is awash with deep yearning to simply be with this person. Close proximity and emotional accessibility and availability, however rudimentary they may be then, capture these innermost desires directed at someone very particular and distinct both in sexual and personality make-up. Simply put, here is a living breathing human being desiring another living breathing human being in all sorts of ways and in a strikingly profound and complex manner.

This rather personal but common experience accentuates the fact that all feelings, thoughts, sensations, wishes, desires, imaginings, and mental images are salient lineaments of desiring, of being attracted to and having fond affection towards a particular person. Sexuality is driven by this interior psychic life and energy that is often punctuated by or expressed in a whole range of inner psychological processes and bodily behavior—from gentle gestures to genital contact. For this reason, sexuality cannot be "construed simply as the desire to engage in sexual acts," although that is part of

7. Spargo, *Foucault and Queer Theory*, 17.

8. Moore, *Question of Truth*, 38

it, "but it is much broader in its scope, embracing activities, and the desire to perform activities, which may go far beyond sexual activity."[9]

Conversations around homosexuality, especially when paired with traditional biblical and theological assertions, usually miss this important point. Here again we see that the personal gets pushed aside in favor of a singular exegetical claim. At best, the discourse becomes reductionistic, and at worst it is a gross distortion of our lived experience. Often this narrative contains a forced dichotomy between sexual orientation or predisposition, on the one hand, and homosexual acts or practices, on the other. The latter is easier to police, and the former just fades into the background. This of course contributed to so much pain and confusion, especially for those trying to align their sexuality with their Christian faith. To make matters worse, these desires in their totality—sexual, psychological, or relational—have been labeled as "intrinsically disordered," "incompatible with Scripture or biblical teaching," and "sinful or unnatural," and those who experience them are considered defective, morally weak, inferior, and disordered heterosexuals. Despite all protestations, there continues to be a singular focus on sexual-genital acts when discussing these issues, which really has to do with regulating and policing what the larger culture has deemed as "nonnormative" sexual behaviors and privileging "normative" expression of sexuality. More so, these types of conversations evoke a whole set of ingrained cognitive and emotional responses resulting in distancing and judging behaviors that keep us further away as the hated outsiders.

Amidst it all, we are now being invited to participate in a whole new level of human engagement marked by shared vulnerability, respect, curiosity, and hospitality towards the other. As recipients of God's radical love, we can begin to create queer spaces where we can model a nonreactive stance and unanxious presence in the hope that, through these rather "strange or unpopular responses," we can envision together what it means to live rightly despite our differences. Our active participation in this restorative work is a way of making God's creative and dynamic wisdom and transformative presence actual, right in the midst of the ruins that is produced by the ongoing social mechanism of exclusion. Such bold act can only emanate from a very secure place—the acknowledgement of our true and inviolable identity as God's Beloved.

9. Moore, *Question of Truth*, 40.

[handwritten margin note: Learned things / HUMAN interactions]

GOD'S BELOVED

One wintery morning found me seated at the back of an Anglican church in Calgary AB, a church I frequented when I was relocated to direct our growing counseling program. That Sunday was like any other Sunday, except for a brief moment of divine surprise that stayed with me until now. A throng of kids marched onto the chancel area for a short time of teaching and blessing. On their way back, a kid of about two to three years old was toddling around with his small little hands clasped onto mom's. As if they were in slow motion, he walked past me with a glee in his eyes, a look of delight that strangely warmed my heart. Unbeknownst to this little kid, that momentary, simple yet profound, unconscious gesture of innocent glance made me feel divinely seen. "God really likes me," I thought to myself with a grin on my face.

I have had similar experiences of being on the receiving end of someone's delight for my mere presence. A display of unabashed welcome hugs and kisses from my family when I come home for a short visit and a look of joy and pleasure from dear friends when we get together for coffee or short walks. There is also this sustained gesture of warmth and appreciation for who I am and the work I do at my previous institution, or when I preach and teach, or simply hang out with my church friends in Calgary Alberta. Of late, an enthusiastic expression of excitement and heartening anticipation was extended to me when I joined the faculty at Garrett Seminary. These seemingly isolated events are stitched together by a common thread of being seen as I am, a delightful regard offered without any conditions, a sense of belongingness that requires no prior stamp of approval.

The immense power of such experiences in making us feel wanted, desired, and affirmed create a deep well of self-acceptance that we can draw from, especially in moments of relative equanimity, or when stung by a sense of inadequacy. But there is another layer or element to this relational exchange that makes me wonder at times, something that usually creeps up on me when pricked by a sense of insecurity. In a world of meritocracy, it is often difficult to differentiate between the regard that is given to us because of what we do and the regard that is offered simply because of who and what we are. The former is a bottomless pit that can never be satiated, and the latter is like a cup that overflows without end.

This I have learned through a conversation I had with Evan, a dear friend of many years. His gracious and accepting accompaniment and childlike attitude became a steady anchor, especially during those critical times when I tried to navigate the challenges of being gay and Christian on top of living and studying in a foreign land. During many seasons of therapy and self-analysis and intense conversations with Evan, I have realized my proclivity to work extra hard on my relationships for fear that if I lax just a tiny bit, I will get cut off from the anchor and find myself on a shifting and unsteady ground. As you can imagine, time spent together with them was riddled with a tinge of anxiety, and therefore has eclipsed even the simple joys these relationships have brought into my life. Yet in the midst of my own internal battle, a gesture of consistent genuine liking slowly cracked my defense to prove my worth through works. And when this shield crumbled, I have discovered being invited to relax, to surrender the impulse to perform and produce to merit acceptance and approval, and to simply be and receive the gratuitous holy regard of another.

There is something profoundly affecting about being seen without feeling judged, of receiving someone else's beholding without the need to hold back, of gradually discovering that this seeing entails an invitation to get past the stifling and often myopic self-evaluations into becoming a person that is of immense value, worth, and possibilities. Recall the incident of the calling of the first disciples of Jesus in Matt 4:18–22 (also recorded in Mark 1:16–20, Luke 5:1–11, and John 1:35–51). In these accounts, we witness the disciples of Jesus responding unequivocally to his call to follow him, leaving behind everything and everyone that defined and constituted their so-called life, relations, and identity. This affirmative stance comes after being "seen" by Jesus, perhaps because of their conviction that he is the promised Messiah, a claim that Jesus himself did not assert. But regardless of their motives and projections, it might be refreshing to give these accounts a second queer look. Only this time, though, we will focus our reflection on the act of seeing and the impact of being noticed, or "eyeballed" in modern parlance, by someone whose authority lies not in force, but in the quiet inversion of social order and power arrangement. Repeatedly in these call narratives, we encounter the phrase "he saw," a sign of Jesus turning his gaze more intently and therefore at the exclusion of others, on certain individuals who are plain and ordinary fishers who would then become fishers of people, and later, apostles. Implicit in this act of beholding someone is perhaps a feeling of affinity with or even a sense of ease, liking, acceptance, and belief in the potential of the other. In fact, neither the in-group fighting for power (Mark 10:35–45) nor their betrayal and abandonment of Jesus (Matt 26:46—28:20) has diminished or disqualified them from becoming the forerunners of the great good news that is Jesus Christ. Such unshakeable and unconditional "holy regard" of Jesus toward his disciples, and by extension towards us queer folks, is a radical display of what it means to be "seen" by God. Jesus saw each of them as they were with such great delight, and he had faith in them, past their craving for power and betrayal, for what they were to become in him and with him. In that exchange, and gradually by following Jesus and being witnesses of the embodiment of God through him, they have received their sense of self or identity. Through the eyes of God in Christ, "eyes that are like us, from alongside, at the same level as us,"[10] they have experienced themselves in a new way, and therefore were able to envision a radical way of living, being, and relating as disciples of Christ.

We see that same divine regard when Jesus interacted with people considered to be on the fringes, and were excluded from society's favor and esteem. Jesus "saw" Levi (Luke 5:27–32) and Zacchaeus (Luke 19:1–10) both tax collectors and outcasts. But that "seeing" yielded a table fellowship, a social statement about Jesus crossing boundaries and intimating a formation of a new community based not on religious or social status but on the grounds of being bearers of divine image. Their encounters with Jesus evinced a transformed life, which I suspect they never saw coming, until Jesus laid eyes on them and saw right through the pattern of desire they have been inducted into by their history and story. Contrast this to the way the Pharisees, teachers of religious law, and others reacted when they "saw" Jesus mingling with these so-called "sinners." They "complained bitterly" (Luke 5:30) and were "displeased and grumbled" (Luke 19:6–7). Their eyes were filled with disdain and their sight full of judgment and in the process were blind to see an inversion of what it means to belong to the Kingdom of God.

That "look" I am sure, is all too familiar for many of us. The way we carry ourselves, the inflection of our voice, or giving voice to our innermost longings or commitments are usually met with looks of disapproval and worse, disgust. And for many we have learned to use the same set of eyes to look at ourselves with disastrous and often life-negating results. Thankfully, this distorted vision can be corrected, for we are being invited to wear a different spectacle, so we can begin to see ourselves and others differently through the very eyes of a loving God.

10. Alison, *On Being Liked*, 108.

THE LOOK IN YOUR EYES

Now, there is nothing profoundly fortuitous about this process—of looking at ourselves through the eyes of another. In fact, this reflective nature is something innate and finds its most primal and vivid expression during early years of our lives. To prove this point, try to observe the interaction between a parent and an infant, and notice how the latter mimics or imitate the subtle gestures, facial expressions, and behaviors of the parent. It is quite astonishing to see the relative ease of this little person to voluntarily match the actions of another without prior training on imitation or language to confirm or explain it.[11] Already laying the groundwork for the mechanism of social learning that gets even more complex and intuitively familiar across human development, this imitative ability is mediated by a mosaic of mirror neuron system in the brain. First discovered in monkeys and then subsequently studied using human subjects, this specific brain circuitry is activated when we observe an action laden with intention and emotion performed by another as if we are the one performing the act itself.[12] This seemingly trivial but delightful mimicry, according to a convergence of evidence across disciplines, demonstrates that "imitation based on neural activity and reciprocal interpersonal behavior is what guides and scaffolds human development from the beginning of life, significantly effecting the emergence and functioning of mental representation, communication and language, empathy, self-other differentiation, and a theory of mind."[13] In other words, imitation or psychological mimesis is foundational to our understanding of the nature of the human condition, and more specifically to our conception of self. Here, there is no self apart from the matrix of relationship of which we are part. We are not separate, independent, self-contained beings, but are brought into being by these relationships and are continued to be formed and informed by these interactions. Not only do we unconsciously and automatically mimic the more obvious bodily gestures of others during our early childhood development, we also imitate their desires, intentions, emotions, and behaviors in like manner over time and without conscious deliberation, giving rise to the "origin and structure of human culture and religion."[14] As will be described in chapter 3, this

11. Garrels, *Mimesis and Science*, 59.
12. Rizzolatti, "Mirror-Neuron System," 169–92.
13. Garrels, "Imitation, Mirror Neurons," 49.
14. Garrels, "Imitation, Mirror Neurons," 49.

human capacity to imitate the other also produces a mimetic crisis that leads to the scapegoating mechanism, a sobering reality to which the queer community is subjected relentlessly. But we are not forever imprisoned by the contagion that is mimetic desire, for we are also called to be imitators of Christ, a process and way of being that is sustained by particular spiritual practices, as discussed more in depth in chapter 4.

Indulge me just a little bit more as I describe further the implication of our imitative capacity within the context of homophobia and how we might resist the internalization of that through intentional refocusing of sight and recasting of our vision based on God's holy regard towards us. The fact that one of our earlier but primary moves as vulnerable little persons is to imitate those whose psychological and physical caretaking we depend on for survival suggest that this "social other precedes us, is prior to us."[15] This social other runs the gamut from persons who are familial or otherwise to larger complex systems such as religion and culture. The most poignant aspect of this is that this social other is not just prior to us, unaffected by our existence, but is intricately involved in bringing us into being—that sort of person that resembles those around us in some fundamental ways. In other words, "who we are is given us by the regard of another."[16]

For most us, we have been inserted into a family, religious, or cultural constellation that have very particular views, usually of a derogatory and demeaning nature about homosexuality. Early into our psycho-sexual development, we get bombarded by these negative and negating messages, both in action and words, which in turn are internalized and become our lifescripts. Inevitably, this leads to disastrous consequences, a self-inflicted violence of all sorts wielded by the social other immersed in homophobic practices and ideologies. Worse, God has been reduced as part of the social other, and is co-opted to legitimize such ungodly acts. But God has got nothing to do with this violence. It is all part of a social mechanism that derives its goodness and creates a sense of belongingness over against another. Our mere presence makes others look and feel good about themselves, and such a false sense of communal belongingness and righteousness are fiercely defended against the intrusion of the excluded other. They become "holy" because of our supposed "unholiness" as queers. To put it another way, we have to be the "bad guys" for them to be the "good and godly collective." We don't have to play that game, however.

15. Alison, *Jesus the Forgiving Victim*, 19.
16. Alison, *Jesus the Forgiving Victim*, 25.

Even though psychological mimesis is impossible to give up, we can start directing our gaze to someone who delights in us as we are, and through that same process of imitation, we begin to see and regard ourselves as God's Beloved. Notice that the preceding discussion resorts to the use of the word "like" to describe God's regard towards us instead of "love." For quite a while now, the word "love" has somewhat lost its transformative power, especially when used to emotionally blackmail the other. This comes in the form of instituting and rewarding heteronormative conformity as the rightful response to the "sacrificial act of love" of Christ on our behalf. In other words, when used in this manner, this supposedly "unconditional love" is conditional through and through, and capitalizes on guilt-tripping that chains queer Christians to psychological insanity and spiritual abuse. Indeed, there is so much baggage or layered expectations with the word "love" that we often hear in the normative discourse on homosexuality. Perhaps, it may be wise at this point to emphasize God "liking us—" delighting in who we are as we are and is pleasurably invested in our own flourishing starting from where we are. In a startling rendering of a core belief about Christ, James Alison writes:

> It seems to me that the doctrine of the incarnation of our Lord, the image of God coming among us as the *likeness* of humans, is a strong statement that the divine regard is one of *liking* us, here and now, as we are. Glad to be with us. And this means that the one who looks at us with love is not just looking at us with a penetrating gaze of utter otherness, but is looking at us with the delight of one who enjoys our company, who wants to be one with us, to share something with us.[17]

God's liking towards us is echoed once again when we think about how Jesus Christ sees and regards his disciples—as his friends (John 15:14–16). In friendship, there is a palpable sense of mutual liking, of feeling relaxed in each other's presence, of wishing the other *shalom*, bearing fruit in every way. In this manner of relating, there is ease and comfort in just being who we are without any pretensions or acting on somebody else's projections. We simply be in the presence of someone who give us our true be-ing. Such delightful and divine regard makes obedience to the law of love an outward expression of an experiential and intimate knowing of being liked by God. Hence, when the undercurrent of "liking" is allowed to resurface in the

---

17. Alison, *On Being Liked*, 107–8.

waves and ways of "loving," we get a fuller, freeing, and abiding sense of what it means to be God's Beloved Queer.

So, every time we find ourselves immersed again in our internalized homophobia, we come up for air and rise! When feel excluded and alienated from our family or oppressed by church and society, we stand next to each other and rise! When we are guilted and then grafted into invasive vines, we reach out to the True Vine and rise! With courage, we rise and poise the ears of our heart to listen attentively to the gentle voice of God, who is not part of the social other, declaring "You are my Beloved child, in whom I am well pleased." Now, take a moment and let these words sink in, allow them to permeate every cell in your body, enlivening and energizing you to become a fierce and fabulous bearer of imago Dei, who calls you Beloved.

TEXTS IN CONTENTION

Much of the debate surrounding the so-called "clobber texts" is significantly informed by differences in hermeneutical entry points. These entry points are never neutral or value-free. We all bring pre-formed ideas that are greatly shaped by the prevailing zeitgeist, particularly around issues of human sexuality. In the case of the discourse on homosexuality within the traditional or conservative evangelical milieu, we often find a belief system that has strong moralistic flavor backed by a peculiar reading of Scripture and sustained by prescriptive social and behavioral practices. For those of us who have lived mostly under the canopy of this religious milieu, these systematized ideas and practices are prior to us, given to us over time by the social other—family, church, and the larger society—which then become part of us, a way of seeing and understanding not just about our sexuality, but also about our sense of worth or value (or lack thereof) and standing before God.

In a Foucauldian fashion, the normative discourse on homosexuality is more than just about a belief system or a way of thinking or producing meaning about our sexuality, or prescribing sexual practices that are deemed (im)proper and (un)godly but ultimately about power relations, of constituting, regulating, governing *our* bodies, mind, and emotional life.[18] The ongoing production of this "body of knowledge" deployed through various means and outlets is a potent force of spreading and maintaining

18. Weedon, *Feminist Practice and Poststructuralist Theory*, 108.

heterosexual hegemonic "power that circulates in the social field and can attached to strategies of domination"[19] over and against the queer community. Within the evangelical domain, this discourse is accorded with a status of truth, of God's truth, because of its supposedly divine origins, while other alternative discourses are conveniently otherized, subjugated, or scapegoated for reasons that will be expounded later on.

Interestingly, the site of resistance is also situated from within this experience of marginality. And it is from this same place that a queer reading of these texts is offered, albeit in an abbreviated form. As an expression of resistance, these alternative readings aim at exposing the hidden mechanism of power and privilege, of domination and subjugation that is intimately intertwined within the texts themselves and then are concealed or camouflaged as divinely ordained when homosexuality is discussed in our context. From the margins, we deconstructed the homophobic discourse with the hope of dismantling the artificial edifice that was used to keep us at a distance.

We begin our queer reading of these texts often claimed to condemn homosexual practices—Genesis 19, Leviticus 18:22, Romans 1:26–27, 1 Corinthians 6:9, and 1 Timothy 1:10—by noting that there is no unproblematic translatable word for homosexual in both the biblical Hebrew or Greek.[20] Hence, it follows that if there is no equivalent for the word homosexual in the language and context in which these texts were written, then it is problematic to claim that a biblical condemnation under the description "homosexual" is possible. Though some of these writers are certainly addressing or are concerned about particular acts or behaviors, there is no clear evidence that they are concerned with them as homosexual. In other words, much of what has been said about homosexuality is actually a forced transposition of a contemporary Western worldview onto other socio-political, cultural and religious contexts that are foreign to us. It is an overlay of a pre-understanding that is meant to support established social and sexual ordering and hierarchy, which in turn conceal or suppress the contextual and transgressive meanings of these texts. The ensuing discussion is an attempt at clearing away these imposed overlays so we can mine what these controversial texts are about.

The destruction of Sodom and Gomorrah in Genesis 19:1–11 is the go-to passage for a sensational, condemnatory, fear-laden commentary

19. Diamond and Quinby, *Feminism and Foucault*, 185.
20. Moore, *Question of Truth*, 66.

about the immorality of "homosexuality." In critiquing this commentary, we start with Genesis 18:1, rather than Genesis 19:1 where the Lord appears to Abraham in the form of three men who he received with generous hospitality (vv. 1–8). This was rewarded by a promise that they will bear a son (vv. 9–15) despite their advanced years. Two then made their way to Sodom, and the one who stayed behind and is introduced in the text as the Lord revealed his plans to go to Sodom to see if what the people were saying about this city is true (v. 20). Then some sort of "bargaining" occurs, with Abraham pleading on behalf of the righteous people in Sodom, with the Lord promising him that the wicked city will not be destroyed if there are even ten good men found in them (vv. 23–32).

What occurs following Abraham's hospitality and display of solidarity in Genesis 18 is closely linked to the all-too-familiar mass killing and destruction of Sodom and Gomorrah with brimstone and fire in Genesis 19, the latter being the focal point of most, if not all, of these traditional readings. But if we follow the text closely, we discover that the two chapters are a juxtaposition between Abraham's hospitality and the egregious inhospitality of the citizens of Sodom. Whereas Abraham (and Lot) opened his home to his visitors, the men of Sodom, both young and old, wanted nothing but to have sex with them (v. 5). This is where the reference to homosexuality is usually made, which is plainly absent in the text. In fact, Lot's plea is not about the immorality of their request—of engaging in homosexual acts—as is commonly believed, but their utter disregard for the fact that these two men are his guests who must be shown honor and respect. To use them for sexual pleasures is to humiliate them, and is exactly the opposite of the generous hospitality Lot and Abraham afforded. Worse, what the men of Sodom actually have in mind here is rape, even gang rape (if we may be so bold here), a form of sexual domination.[21] Thus, it can be surmised here that the sin of Sodom and Gomorrah is not the immorality of homosexual desire run amok, but in their gross failure to extend hospitality, and for engaging in attempted gang rape. By extension, it is also a "sexual form of inhospitality and a sexual insult to God,"[22] since the two men are the instantiation of the divine. Again, there is simply not a judgment on homosexuality that we can find in this text.

The two texts in Leviticus, namely chapters 18:22 and 20:13, contain no story arc from which to extract moral teachings, like the ones the above.

21. Moore, *Question of Truth*, 71.
22. Moore, *Question of Truth*, 72.

What is made plain in these two verses is an injunction regarding male same-sex activity (not their female counterparts), which is considered an abomination (18:22) and is punishable by death (20:13). At first glance, these passages are easy theological clickbait in favor of Christian condemnation of homosexuality. So, it seems.

The alternative reading of this text takes off from exactly the same point where traditional reading makes its case: "You shall not lie with a male as with a woman, it is an abomination."[23] The interpretive move we make here is to take this rather plain moral injunction and situate it within the larger social and sexual hierarchy in Israel. In this society, there is a clear hierarchical sexual ordering and distinction between men and women. Men, as the dominant sex, take center stage in all domestic and social affairs, while women are seen as the possession of men, their importance contingent on being someone else's property on the same level as everything men have at their disposal.[24] And since this hierarchy is perceived to have a divine origin, every violation is considered tantamount to an outright rebellion against God.[25] But there's more to this social arrangement than meets the eye. The firmly established pyramidal structure has a wider reach that covers even the most personal and sexual relations between a man and a woman. The dominant stature of the man carries over to this domain expressed through penetrative penile-vaginal intercourse with the subordinate woman, a "symbolic taking and giving of possession."[26] Hence, what is considered a violation here is not male same-sex activity per se, but the sexual penetration of one man by another, of putting him in a subordinate and inferior position like that of a woman, of taking possession. In this context, this is considered a clear infraction of a divinely ordered social and sexual hierarchy as created by God, and by extension a direct assault to God's own authority.

When pressed further to give account to other biblical passages that provide moral prohibitions against homosexuality, traditionalists appeal to Romans 1 without hesitation.

Its position in the biblical canon, in comparison to the Old Testament texts we just considered, is considered significant because it is part of the

23. Lev 3:18, RSV.
24. Moore, *Question of Truth*, 74.
25. Moore, *Question of Truth*, 76.
26. Moore, *Question of Truth*, 77.

new dispensation inaugurated by Jesus Christ.[27] The phrase "the Bible is quite clear . . ." then carries much more weight when followed by a particular reading of this text. Gay Christians on the receiving end of this experience "deep emotional and spiritual annihilation, something inflicting paralysis," a real text of terror.[28] The major source of this reaction is the unqualified condemnation of sexual behaviors of both men and women which we call "homosexuality" in modern terms. Here, both sexes are implicated, compared to the one-sided male-focused prohibitions we saw on the Genesis and Leviticus texts. Yet, just like the foregoing, what seems obvious as a sacred injunction against homosexuality in this pericope is not that obvious after all.

If we widen our lens to capture the surrounding context in which the passage was written, we find the apostle Paul addressing not same-sex activity, but the idolatrous practices of the gentiles,[29] a large segment of the populace who do not worship the one true God, the God of Israel. Their greatest sin, which merited a whole host of punishment (vv. 21–25), is impiety and injustice, those who suppress the truth (v. 18): "though they knew God, they neither glorified him as God nor gave thanks to him, but their thinking became futile and their foolish hearts were darkened." The transgression that is leveled against them is their willful disregard for the truth, of making a mockery of God's unequalled standing as the Creator by bending their knees before God's creatures.

Further, what gives this reading plausibility is the fact that the polemic contained in verses 18–26 is a very common Jewish argument against pagan practices, something that Paul and his readers were very familiar with.[30] And it is because "pagan people became involved in the idolatrous cults that then they were led to get involved in passions which did them no honor."[31] These pagan cultic practices include temple prostitution and rites involving frenzied orgies where men are being penetrated and often culminating in some of them castrating themselves and becoming eunuchs and priests of some deity.[32]

---

27. Moore, *Question of Truth*, 86.
28. Alison, *Undergoing God*, 123.
29. Moore, *Question of Truth*, 7.
30. Alison, *Undergoing God*, 133.
31. Alison, *Undergoing God*, 133.
32. Alison, *Undergoing God*, 133.

The other critique offered to the traditional reading of Romans 1 has something to do with subdividing these texts into chapters and verse numbers, a heuristic and helpful device for modern readers. However, something really vital about the intention of the text gets lost in the process, like what we have here in this passage. If we take out these numerical assignments, we find the beginning pages of the epistle ends with a fitting conclusion with the words "Therefore" (see Romans 2:1). So, while the apostle Paul is addressing the idolatry of the gentile world, no one is off the hook, Jews and gentile alike. Everyone is implicated in following the same pattern of desire in which this world operates, "filled with every kind of wickedness, evil, greed and depravity" (vv. 29–31). Lest the audience of the apostle falls fully into the trap of "us" (holy Jews) vs. "them" (sinful gentiles), he said, "Therefore, you have no excuse, you who pass judgment on someone else, for at whatever point you judge another, you are condemning yourself, because you who pass judgment do the same things."

The remaining two verses—1 Corinthians 6:9 and 1 Timothy 1:10— contain the Greek words *malakoi* and *arsenokotoi*, which pose a great deal of a challenge for translators. But we can be certain of one thing: these two words are not the equivalent of the modern-day word "homosexual." The word malakoi can simply means "soft," which is often associated with the feminine, either in terms of comportment as in effeminate or feminine sexual behavior.[33] Given the Hellenistic emphasis on the masculine, it seems probable that what Paul disapproves of points to the "softness in men," on being passive, of not taking on the social role and expectation of having brute strength, self-control, and virility, and not some kind of homosexual behavior. This inversion is considered to be a serious moral offence and therefore deserving of societal contempt.

The word *arsenokotoi* has clear sexual overtones in the same vein as the prohibition given in Leviticus 18:22, of men in the dominant penetrative position performing some kind of a sex act with men who assume the feminized submissive (*malakoi*) role.[34] Confirmation of this plausible reading can be found in the writing of Paul's contemporary Philo and his condemnation of the practice of pederasty, of taking on younger men and corrupting them for their own sexual gratification.[35] With these two words placed side by side, we can infer that what Paul seems to be addressing

33. Moore, *Question of Truth*, 107.
34. Moore, *Question of Truth*, 108.
35. Moore, *Question of Truth*, 109.

in this text is not homosexual relationships or homosexual practices per se, but sexual practices that go against the established social and sexual hierarchy, of men actively involved in feminizing other men (*arsenokotoi*) and those who take on that role willingly (*malakoi*).

In 1 Timothy 1:10, we find the same word *arsenokotoi* appear again, along with the list of people who live their lives contrary to sound teaching. The meaning ascribed to this word is similar to our reading of the Corinthian passage, but with further elaboration. Some interpreters relate the word "slave traders" to *arsenokotoi*, those people who kidnap young men to work as prostitutes in brothels. It is possible, then, that Paul might be speaking of *arsenokotoi* as "clients of brothels who bought the sexual services of boy slaves."[36] Again, these last two texts we have considered do not offer a definitive sacred condemnation again homosexual relationships or practices, as most traditional readings claim in their normative discourse.

The queer interpretations of the so-called "clobber texts" provided here differ radically from what we are used to hearing. With their unique contexts appearing on the background, we get to see the foreground more clearly—that the texts' plausible meanings have more to do with issues of inhospitality, idolatry, attempted gang rape, inversion of ancient but established societal and sexual hierarchy, willful disregard for truth, and the problematic pairing of domination and subjugation. These transgressions are not merely directed at another human being, some sort of human (male)-to-human (male) infractions. They are blatant violations ultimately directed at God, a clear subversion of what these writers believed to be the created order.

Fast forward to modern times, the layering of a modern concept of homosexuality to account for the meaning of the texts written at a time far removed from contemporary realities is a function of the scapegoat mechanism. Using these texts to condemn homosexuality is a cover-up, a convenient way of concealing culpability for acts, either of personal or institutional nature, committed against others and God and, in the process, it secures for them unanimity and social belonging. We will delve into this form of sacred violence in subsequent chapters.

But during this process of unlearning the reading habits we have picked up from the social other regarding these texts, let us not forget Paul's admonition in Romans 2:1 and be mindful of our own proclivity in making quick judgments on others that often blinds us from recognizing our own

---

36. Moore, *Question of Truth*, 112.

distorted vision, as well. Integral to adjusting—better yet, correcting our field of vision—is going inward, reacquainting ourselves with our interior psychological life, and discovering glimpses of what makes us human on the same level as everyone else.

CHAPTER TWO

The Interior Landscape

"I JUST WANT SIMPLY to be loved and accepted," Brian cried out. He came out to me when we were both in graduate studies decades ago. Tears came streaming down his face as he narrated his story, particularly his struggles of reconciling his homosexuality with his Christian faith. It was a story that mirrored my own, and his anguish seemed like a chorus belted out by many. As a gesture of deep love for my dear friend, I embraced him and whispered the words, "I know." In an instant, we saw each other in a different way, and the isolation that we felt those many years was bridged by our shared longing or need for love and acceptance as we are.

There are many gay Christians, especially those belonging to conservative evangelical churches, who experience this kind of dissonance in isolation. The fear of getting "found out" is excruciatingly real, the repercussions often unbearable and all-encompassing. When the proposal for this book was accepted, the immediate response was, "Are you ready to lose everything you hold dear—your relationships, career, status, and stability?" The excitement I felt for having been given the opportunity to publish a book of this nature had suddenly been doused by an ominous, yet fair and realistic warning. I have seen too many gay Christians get stripped of pretty close to everything when all they want to do is to be themselves, authentically.

We all have been in situations where we hear people make condemning pronouncements about homosexuality from such places as the pulpit, classrooms, informal gatherings, even at home. And in most cases, we would come away from these encounters feeling angry, confused, shamed, dismissed, afraid, silenced, scrutinized, and dissected by those prying eyes whose vision of our humanity has more to do with their conditioned fear and prejudices. Even further, these declarations are often fraught with "god sayings" masquerading as "gospel truths" that keep us at a distance, shamed and guilt-ridden for simply existing as we are. The phrase "the Bible says" is dispensed with such certitude that it shuts down any possibility for genuine encounter and dialogue regarding an aspect of our humanity that is fundamentally and intimately integral to who we are.

Yet in the midst of a cacophony of voices and unsettling emotions that bubble up inside of me during these encounters, I have also become acquainted with this faint and gentle whisper that reminded me of my true origin and source of regard—that "I am God's Beloved son." Faint though it may be, these words that refuse to die down became my lifeline in moments of confusion and protest, an inner divine witness that is also a witness to the scars of my wounded heart. And even during moments of felt absence, the divine presence remains unperturbed and unthreatened. So, I have learned and am still learning to hold tight to this bestowed identity no matter how strong the force is, both internal and external, that tries to pull me away from it. "On Christ, the solid rock I stand, all other ground is sinking sand,"[1] says a line from a hymn that captures quite poignantly my heart's intent. It is from this place of graced security and unshakeable truth that I offer these reflections, which I hope will make good fodder for ongoing self-reflection, exploration, and encouragement.

The longing for love and acceptance, as Brian so intensely expressed, is not unique to us (though we feel it more strongly, I believe). It is deeply human and therefore shared by all. It orients us towards each other and calls forth within us our innate capacity to love and be loved. However, there is more to this longing than meets the eye, and the well from which this came is deep. Extracting its depth and significance requires that we go beyond the familiar terrain of theology to enter into a dialogue with the discipline of psychology and discover for ourselves another path that I hope will lead us to greater self-awareness and acceptance, without any apology.

Humans need more than just the proverbial daily bread to live, thrive, and flourish. They also require the fulfillment of specific and basic

---

1. See the hymn by Edward Mote, "My Hope Is Built on Nothing Less," which is in the public domain.

psychological needs to be able to develop well and to experience and sustain good mental health. Exactly what these needs are have been the subject of many psychological theories and research.[2] But none came closer to a crystalized, comprehensive, and empirically based understanding of these basic needs than that of Seymour Epstein's theory of human personality[3]. Indulge me for a moment with this rather conceptual exploration. I will do my best to flesh it out by describing this theory through the lens of our experiences. According to Epstein, humans are driven or orient their lives towards the fulfillment of the following four basic psychological needs—1) a need for attachment or relatedness; 2) a need for orientation and control; 3) a need for self-esteem enhancement; and 4) a need to maximize pleasure and minimize distress. Fulfillment of these basic needs contributes to human flourishing. Conversely, repeated and ongoing frustrations or violations of these needs result in impairments in psychological functioning, compromised health, and diminished quality of life.

Sadly, the reasons for their non-fulfillment are many, and too devastating even to enumerate here. But for most gay people, the repeated frustrations or violations of such basic human needs are more pronounced and quite unsettling because they stem not only as punishments for our supposed "immoral acts" but fundamentally as a form of chastisement for our "flawed nature, character, or essences." It is not simply "what we do" that they find problematic, but it is "who we are" that they find detestable. In other words, being gay means not having the right to pursue or fulfill that which makes us essentially human. Now that is a lot to take in. So, before we get ahead of ourselves here, it would be wise to describe each of these four basic psychological needs and then come back to this point later on.

A NEED FOR ATTACHMENT

Has there been a time in your life when you were not in a relationship of any kind with anyone, ever at all? I am pretty certain that that would be quite impossible even to imagine, given the role of relationships in our maturation process. Have you ever wondered what it would be like not to depend on anyone for anything? Again, that would be quite unthinkable, I suspect, since to a great extent we arrive at this stage or juncture of life because we were or are still dependent on these relationships. How much influence

2. Grawe, *Neuropsychotherapy*, 167.

3. Epstein, *Cognitive-Experiential Theory*, 49–58.

do you think early relationships have over your life right now? When we reflect on these questions and begin to trace our initial steps back to our early years, we will discover soon enough the sheer force of these primary relational dynamics or exchange in shaping and molding who we are and how we live our lives, even to this day. In short, from the very beginning, it is human nature to seek out, depend on, and be in close proximity with another human being whose quality of response to these emerging needs can either release or thwart our potential to be fully human.

Attachment, as it is called, is a basic psychological need. Our beginnings are marked with a gesture to reach out or make contact with another human being, usually our caregivers, for survival and nourishment, physically and psychologically conceived. We are wholly dependent on these attachment figures for daily sustenance, physical safety, empathic attunement, unconditional love, and positive regard. Without them, our world disintegrates, and we grow emaciated in fundamentally psychological (not solely in literal) ways.

How others respond to these pressing needs is critical to our development, and their caring presence and attunement (or lack thereof) creates an imprint on how we see ourselves, others, and the world we live in. John Bowlby,[4] a British psychiatrist, offers a penetrating description of a relational dynamic that carries well into different stages across the lifespan. According to him, the experience of a near, responsive, and emotionally available attachment figure impresses a sense of trust and security in the inner world of the child. When optimally provided and created, the child is less likely to experience chronic and often debilitating anxiety that is usually associated with or observed among those who experience consistent attachment ruptures. The expectancies or beliefs (or inner working models) that develop out of this relational exchange during this critical period are carried over into adulthood and are relatively unchanged.[5] To put this differently, the way we navigate our current interpersonal worlds mirrors what we have learned or picked up on an unconscious level during these early relationships. Hence, not only is attachment necessary for our survival, but the quality of attachment also determines in a very profound manner the sort of relationship or people we are drawn towards (or avoid).

Brian's cry for love and acceptance, for an attachment experience that affirmed his humanity without conditions, was a manifestation of a deep

4. Epstein, *Cognitive-Experiential Theory*, 49–58.
5. Epstein, *Cognitive-Experiential Theory*, 49–58.

longing and need that had not been met for most of his life. This unmet need became even more palpable when he came out to his parents. In order to survive in this world and to taste a semblance of connection with others, he had learned to live in the closet or hide his sexuality from them for fear of rejection, exclusion, and isolation. In a sense, he lived a "split-off or fragmented life" for the sake of survival, inclusion and belongingness, only to find himself so far off and disconnected from his true self. Consequently, he developed a pervasive feeling of insecurity and inadequacy within himself and a tentativeness to relate with others the way he wanted to—authentic, honest, and free. Anxiety had become his constant companion expressed in restlessness, apprehension, and avoidance. Often this anxiety turns into anger, sadness, and shame; the latter he described as a "hole" so wide and so deep he would cocoon in his apartment for days on end. This was his way of hiding from the world so he could shed off the mask he had been wearing for so long. Though this solitary move provided momentary solace, he also found it overwhelming because he was confronted with what had become his core belief: "I am not deserving of love." Without a doubt, he knew why!

Brian's anxious relational style is only one of the attachment patterns identified by Bowlby's collaborator Mary Ainsworth.[6] I will try to delineate these patterns briefly in the hope that it will provide some framework from which to understand some aspects of ourselves and the quality of relationships we have, then and now. The landmark study called "Strange Situation" involved children between ages eleven to twenty months and a caregiver. In this procedure, each child is observed playing for twenty-one minutes while caregivers or strangers enter and leave the room. This scenario aims to mirror the flow of the familiar and unfamiliar presence of people in most children's lives. The situation varies in well-calibrated levels of stressfulness, and the child's response to this "strange situation" are observed. Four recurring attachment styles have emerged from this study.

Secure Attachment Style

Children react with distress when separated from their mother and seek her closeness upon reunion. When contact is achieved and reestablished, they display keen and playful curiosity about their surroundings. The relational dynamic evident here is one of basic trust towards the caregiver and security in knowing that an absence will soon be followed by return. This

6. Epstein, *Cognitive-Experiential Theory*, 49ff.

relational dance is one of many building blocks of a child's good attachment experience towards his/her primary relationship.

I believe that gay individuals (or anyone for that matter) who have shown great resilience in the midst of great adversity, in this case in the form of homophobia, discrimination, rejection of all kinds, judgment, and spiritual abuse, are more likely to have been raised in a trusting, safe, and loving environment, a "life and love laboratory," so to speak. Rare though they may be, these kinds of relationships do exist. They do still experience a whole gamut of unpleasant and negative emotions, but have developed wherewithal to regulate and not get overpowered by them. After all, no one is shielded from the pain of getting pushed to live in marginality, but often these good attachment experiences are sufficient enough to be our buffer when pelted with discriminatory acts. Amidst all these, they often exhibit abiding self-confidence or self-belief when dismissed and excluded, eager to reach out to others for support and encouragement, display empathy and compassion towards themselves and the welfare of others, and they continue to harvest fruits of mental well-being, regardless of life's many bumps and turns. Indeed, this is a testament to their resilience, an outcome of emerging from an enriched environment where "good enough" attachment experiences are dispensed without conditions and relational ruptures are repaired, among others.

Insecure Attachment Style: Avoidant

In a sense, this particular behavioral response is the opposite of those who are securely attached. When separation and reunion occur, children with insecure attachment styles tend to avoid any need for contact, nor would they show signs of distress, at least externally, when separated from their caregivers. Such avoidance or detachment is an unconscious defense against the possibility of getting their psychological need for connection frustrated again. Here, the relational dynamic at play between the child and parental dyad is one of repeated and prolonged absence, outright refusal, or dismissal to respond caringly and timely to the child's need for connection or attachment.

I have seen how this pattern of relating wreaks havoc in the lives of couples, gay or straight, that I have worked with in therapeutic settings. The lack of emotional intimacy that couples experience is partly a result of their difficulty or inability to be vulnerable with each other. The fear of contact that is felt and learned early on in childhood overrides their need to connect, leaving both of them isolated, disengaged, alone, and lonely. Intimacy is seen as a threat, as opposed to a gift that can be shared and used to forge a much deeper, enlivening, and mutually satisfying relationship. This too can happen in other forms of relationships where emotional access and availability is tightly defended in favor of superficiality and convenience.

Insecure Attachment Style: Anxious

Children with this pattern tend to display a very tense, worried, and apprehensive behavior when confronted with separation. Such a highly aroused state gives way towards an aggressive and ambivalent bid for contact—rejecting the reunion, while at the same time clamoring for closeness, even clingy at times. These intense emotional fluctuations overwhelm the child to the point of disinterest towards other stimuli or persons present in the environment. The precursor to this, of course, is quite evident. The parent-child dynamic in this instance is marked by unpredictability, intrusiveness, and mis-attunement to the needs of the dependent one in the dyad. Brian's story is riddled with these experiences early on. To my estimation, his parents have not had good attachments themselves, and therefore did not know how to respond appropriately to Brian's emerging and constant need for connection when he was growing up. The ambivalence turned into intrusiveness when he disclosed his sexuality with them later on. Given this constellation, Brian struggled with not knowing appropriate boundaries when he was overwhelmed by feeling of loneliness, isolation, anger, and withdrawal, when expressed needs for connection are unrequited.

Insecure Attachment Style: Disorganized

By far, this is the most disconcerting behavioral response observed by Ainsworth and her colleagues. The separation and subsequent reunion with caregivers evoke a bizarre, confused, fearful, and disoriented response in a handful of these children. This is often a result of a frightening or abusive relationship of physical, emotional, and sexual natures with the primary attachment figure. We now refer to these experiences as early childhood developmental trauma. The effects of such a harrowing experience are many—clinical depression, various forms of personality disorders, substance abuse, and the like—and they seem intractable or quite resistant to psychological treatment or interventions.

All these may sound a bit too abstract and academic. So, let me drive home the point I am trying to make. Our need for attachment or for a relationship that is marked by unconditional love and genuine liking is a basic psychological need that all human beings have regardless of one's sexual orientation. When this need is satiated, it creates a feeling of "love-worthiness" that get internalized and metamorphosed into a sense of self-belief and agency. This then releases the potential to not just survive but to thrive and flourish in an increasingly changing and demanding world. Conversely, when this need is not met consistently, it creates a cavernous void that drives people into certain adaptive actions or behaviors that cover the emptiness inside, and often result in ill health all around.

For gay people, expressing this attachment need even at its most rudimentary level is often met with disdain, rejection, and judgment, and worse, cruelty and violence by some of their very close circle of relationships. Still further, within Christian groups, these judgments and condemnations are often swift, with the usual biblical justifications that run counter to the professed gospel message of love and compassion. Instead of offering a healing and welcoming space where wounds are soothed and repaired, a mechanism of exclusion wins out, causing more damage and trauma to an already afflicted soul. Instead of acknowledging gay Christians as fellow image-bearers of God, whose sacred value and worth mirrors those of others, we often get defaced and demonized, prayed over, or sent to reparative treatment facilities to be "straightened up." Simply, we are seen as undeserving of the fundamental psychological need for attachment, love, and acceptance. And if extended at all, it usually comes at a great price, that is, we need to become someone other than ourselves. In these life-negating conditions, inauthenticity gets us at the door, conformity in belief secures us a place among many, and unanimity acquires us social standing and belongingness. At least, that is the rule, sometimes unspoken and at other times legislated, by those who are more invested in erecting walls than widening its circles to include all. Many of us, if not all, have fallen prey to this social arrangement at one point or another in our lives, and for adaptive and survival reasons. So, there is no judgment and there is no shame, if and when that has been or is our situation. We too are only human, in search of a home that will shelter us from the torrent of isolation, loneliness, and insecurity. Sometimes we settle for a mere semblance of a home rather than wander around alone and disconnected. Alas, there is another path that has been cleared for us, another way of securing a sense of belongingness or attachment that only requires one thing, that is, to be truly ourselves as we are and not someone else. And that offer comes from God who-is-not-like-other-gods, who really likes and delights in us as we are. It may feel far-fetched for those of us accustomed to experiencing a punitive judgmental god that is a distorted copycat of the One True God.

A NEED FOR ORIENTATION AND CONTROL

One of the presenting problems I encounter frequently in therapeutic contexts is the issue of control. "I am losing control," or "I don't have any control," or "someone is trying to control me" are aches I hear from many of these clients. These aches express themselves in chronic stress and debilitating anxiety. It impacts clients' daily life, relationships, and occupations, and compromises their physical and mental well-being. For many counselors, the paths to healing are myriad and therapy usually centers around helping clients either give up their need for too much control or take control back into their life.

The incidence of individuals struggling with these issues is not unique to the counseling population. It is likely that there are more people from all walks of life who share this burden. It is also possible that these laments betray something far more fundamental than we realize or care to admit. That the fear of "losing control, or not being in control, or that someone tries to or is controlling me" is actually a violation or non-fulfillment of yet another basic psychological need. Approaching this as an unfulfilled need, as opposed to a personal deficiency, has far-reaching implications, not only in clinical practice, but in life in general, particularly when it comes to the issue of homosexuality.

The need for orientation and control is inextricably linked with the need for attachment, especially during the critical early years. The ever-unfolding dependency needs of the young and the timely and attuned response of the caregiver is the beginning of a lifelong journey towards meeting the need for "positive control experiences and self-efficacy."[7] The physical and psychological holding the caregiver provides in response to the child's bid for attention and caretaking impresses upon the child the sense that he or she can use his or her behaviors (e.g., crying or reach-

7. Grawe, *Neuropsychotherapy*, 214.

ing out) to achieve desired actions (e.g., satiate hunger or satisfy the need to be in proximity with the caregiver). Thus, the need for control can be understood as a "need to be able to perform some action that is important for the attainment of personal goals,"[8] another key component of healthy maturational development. When these needs are not met consistently, a feeling of disorientation and lack of control and self-agency ensue, obvious symptoms for those having difficulty to cope with problems in living.

As we grow and develop, the need for control becomes more complex in that it presupposes an accurate and realistic appraisal of what is going within us and around us. Am I in control of my own interior world? Does my perception of reality correspond with the "larger household of reality"[9] shared by many? Is there congruence between my interior world, those basic needs and aspirations I have for myself and what is available externally to meet such needs, to become the kind of person I desire to be? These questions are simply our way of expressing our need for orientation, of wanting to have clarity on and opportunity for attaining our needs and life's goals.[10] When this need is met, that is, when the interior world coalesces with the benevolent external world, it sends a message that says, "you matter, your needs matter, and we are here to support your well-being." In turn, this produces positive emotions, strengthens self-agency, and encourages greater engagement with life in general.

This begs the question: What has been the experience of gay Christians when it comes to fulfilling the need for orientation and control? Not too encouraging, of course. Let me paint a scenario that happens all too frequently, sad to say. For many of us, becoming acutely aware of our sexuality brings a mixture of visceral and emotional response. Delight is not the first reaction. Fear is! And in an environment that is still generally hostile, averse, and inhospitable to our sexuality, this process of self-discovery is overwhelmingly daunting, to say the least. Fears of rejection, exclusion, and even expulsion are real threats. The longing for acceptance and belongingness in an unresponsive environment does not disappear. It intensifies. It is like coming to a fork in the road feeling stuck, immobilized, and uncertain about what path to take because whatever road one decides to travel on always entails a great deal of sacrifice. Indeed, claiming or embracing (or denying) one's sexuality each exact a high price that most of us are not

8. Grawe, *Neuropsychotherapy*, 213.

9. Volf, *Human Flourishing*, 14.

10. Volf, *Human Flourishing*, 14.

equipped to handle because of pressures of all kinds that hem us in from all sides.

In fact, in most cases we often feel at a loss, disoriented and confused about how to navigate this predominantly straight world that has tentacles everywhere. There is a clash within and without fighting for dominance and attention. On the one hand, we experience our erotic desires as entirely our own, emerging from our core, that part of ourselves that is authentically us and ours. On the other, we have heard messages, injunctions, and judgments that are strong, direct, and often negative emerging from outside of us and are spoken with such certainty by the social other—family, culture and society, and religion. As such, we are in a state of disorientation and internal fragmentation because we are differently oriented than most people around us. A war that we did not initiate is constantly waged, and we are its own casualty. Because of this pervasive conflict, we often feel a sense of not being in control of our own bodies and subjective experiences, unclear about who we are and must become, and apprehensive about what the future might bring. All this conspires against a free and fluid pursuit of personal goals that are meant to flourish us and authenticates who we are at the very core of our being. So, once again we face yet another obstacle: the fulfillment of the basic psychological need for orientation and control is thwarted or blocked because of our sexuality, an integral part of our humanity.

The blockage seems formidable, doesn't it? Perhaps, for some of us, we have caved in to the straight world or resisted its hegemonic power. Either way, it cost us our lives in varying degrees. Yet, without sounding trite, you are loved passionately and unreservedly by Another Other, our God who is for us and over against nothing or no one at all. This love frees us from the shackles of doubt, either self-induced or imposed from the outside, and invites and releases us to make actual our innate capacity to be agents of our lives so that we can begin to pursue that which brings joy, satisfaction, and happiness, not only for ourselves but those around us, even in the midst of a world that remains inhospitable towards us. I say this because I still believe that God's love and God's queer ways can never be thwarted by any human effort to contain it.

43

A NEED FOR SELF-ESTEEM ENHANCEMENT AND SELF-ESTEEM PROTECTION

Let me ask you a couple of questions, and you can respond by indicating how strongly you agree or disagree with each statement:

1. Generally, I am satisfied with myself.

2. I feel I do not have much to be proud of.

3. I feel that I am a person of worth.

4. All in all, I am inclined to feel that I am a failure.

5. I take a positive attitude toward myself.[11]

Our responses to these questions paint a picture of ourselves that either unsettles us or make us feel quietly and humbly self-assured. If we indicate agreement with statements one, three, and five, and disagree with statements two and four, then it is safe to say that we have a positive regard or outlook about ourselves. And as experience would have it, those who have good-enough self-regard tend to move through life with its many twists and turns resilient, hopeful, curious, inspirited, and open. Conversely, those who suffer from low self-esteem tend to see themselves, others, and the world with apprehension, fear, and mistrust, and are stricken by endless self-doubt and resignation. This drive to feel good about ourselves, that we are worthy of love and capable of engaging life in satisfying and growth-inducing ways, is the basic law of human existence.[12] Hence, failure to meet this need inhibits our capacity to live life in its fullness.

But how does one achieve a positive self-regard or esteem? As you might have expected, this is not something that develops in isolation. The seed is planted in the fertile ground of the parent-child relational matrix, where the quality of attachment correlates with the level of self-esteem. An attuned, attentive, and secure attachment experience communicates to the child that he or she is loveworthy. The excitement and great delight expressed in the eyes of the caregiver when he or she sees the child, the warm embrace and gentle kiss, the tender loving care extended especially when ill, the unhurried attention when playing peekaboo, and not to mention the provision of basic needs for nourishment, shelter, and safety, all contribute to this feeling of being wanted, cherished, loved, and liked. When

11. Rosenberg, *Society and the Adolescent*, 17–18.
12. Becker, *Structure of Evil*, 157.

consistently offered over time, these seeds of love grow and flower into a positive self-image, a sense of security and individuality, and a burgeoning graciousness and welcoming attitude towards others, just like how he or she was made to feel by his or her own close circle of relationships.

Imagine yourself experiencing the opposite of a healthy attachment upbringing. So, instead of bathing in love, you get immersed in constant rejection or neglect; instead of being delighted upon, you get dismissed and pushed aside; and instead of feeling valued, you feel worthless. What sort of a self or identity do you think emerges from this wasteland of unfulfilled needs and disconnection? And is there even a self to speak of? What if, in the midst of such impoverished state, you also are now just discovering or are dealing with your sexuality as a gay person? In other words, whatever vestige remains of a shaky sense of self is now threatened by yet another ominous feeling of further wounding and pain because of your sexuality.

Stuck between a rock and a hard place, and with limited options in sight, the instinctual need for survival kicks in. Engaging in behaviors that can ease or numb the pain of feeling "unloveworthy" becomes irresistibly enticing. Staying in the closet to stay connected becomes a conduit of some sort to gain acceptance and belongingness. At times the only way to survive is to come out of the closet only to find oneself bereft of homes, relations, even occupations. And tragically, there are others who retreat from the battle completely with devastating consequences. It is no surprise, then, to witness a disturbingly high prevalence of depression and suicide attempts and other mental health conditions, especially among the young members of the queer community. Surrounded by disapproving milieu and a pervasive internal sense of worthlessness, we see a collapse of a self that tears at the very core of our humanity.

But there is good news. The problem of low self-esteem, though it seems intractable, can be reversed. The internal rupture created by early relationships can be repaired via the same pathway—a particular kind of relationship that is marked by acceptance, deep empathy and compassion, and genuine liking. It is often hard to imagine that this is at all possible, especially after experiencing the opposite from those closest to us. We may not even recognize the gesture when it is offered to us because it is unfamiliar, and therefore breeds more mistrust in people's intentions, or because the voice of our internal critic and judge is so loud that it drowns out the gentle invitation and loving attention of others towards us. There is no shame when this happens, for it is part of the narrative we have learned or have been conditioned to live by.

The story is not finished yet. In fact, many of us have found life-giving relationships, sometimes in unexpected ways. Or these relationships have found us, sheltered us, and made us feel loved, liked, and fully embraced as we are. They have somehow become our surrogate parents, graced and gentle shepherds of our interior life, and spiritual guides that led us to a place of nourishment to feed our famished souls and esteemed us unconditionally. But these gifts are ours to share as well. As recipients of such hospitality and generosity, we are empowered to extend these circles of love and security. We accomplish this by accompanying those who are taking their first courageous step of letting themselves be known by another, for we believe that it is within the context of relationships—relational and devotional—that a rebirth of the self is made possible. For many of them, being vulnerable with another will take time, as their hurt is deep. So we wait patiently, sometimes in our quiet reassuring presence, and sometimes with words of encouragement. When we create this holding environment, they will soon rediscover their worthiness and uniqueness as a human being, loved and liked by God and by those who can see the divine image in them.

A NEED TO MAXIMIZE PLEASURE AND MINIMIZE DISTRESS

I am curious to know the last time you feel good all-around—physically, emotionally, mentally, relationally, sexually, and spiritually? What kind of situation or context gave rise to this pleasant and positive state? How often do you experience it? What do you believe to be the common ingredients that make up pleasurable and unpleasurable experiences? In other words, what makes someone feel happy and satisfied?

Answers to these questions are relatively easy to conjure. Why? Because the need for pleasure maximization and lessening distress is proven to be the most obvious of all basic psychological needs. These experiences are readily felt on a physical level and lend themselves easily to self-observation.[13] Going back to our formative years, crying and other similar gestures are bodily expressions of our distress, as well as our bids for immediate attention and relief. That whole repertoire of body enactments is oriented towards the minimization of unpleasant feeling-states. On the other

13. Grawe, *Neuropsychotherapy*, 240.

end of the spectrum, there are also those moments of sheer joy and play-ful demeanor when we are engaged in pleasurable activities (e.g., playing peekaboo with a caregiver), which also orient us towards the attainment of pleasant feeling-states. These critical experiences lay the groundwork for our neverending search for happiness, which is a state of subjective well-being that humans strive for.

But what exactly do we mean by happiness? And why do we long so much to experience it? In simpler terms, happiness is a life well-lived. It goes beyond the pleasure principle (though it is a part of it), and has to do more with finding meaning, purpose, and coherence in life. To be happy is to experience alignment between personal goals (e.g., having a clear sense of one's identity and purpose in life) and current perceptions of the world (e.g., the world as a safe place to live out this purpose) without any compet-ing and conflicting intentions.[14] When these collide, we experience positive emotions of delight and pleasure, as well as the abiding sense of peace and wholeness, akin to the experience of "flow."[15]

Now, that is not necessarily how most people understand happiness. We usually conceive of it strictly in terms of pursuing pleasures in life, the hedonic way, that make us feel good. Oftentimes such pursuit gets so self-indulgent, the pleasurable experiences short-lived and obsessive to the exclusion of other goals. Finding the next fix takes center stage, which often leads to devastating consequences (e.g., addictions). And in a highly stressed society such as ours, the allure for immediate or instant gratifica-tion to fend off increasing demands, conflicts, and pressures of life becomes so irresistible that we could not help but cave in at times, only to find our-selves in the most unpleasurable and distressful state imaginable.

Ancient tradition sees happiness in a different light which we are now retrieving and redressing for contemporary usage. For them, it is about being authentic, engaged, and connected to a transcendent cause, like the flourishing of all sentient beings. This is the eudaemonic way, as ancient philosophers have coined it, and it embraces and accepts a certain degree of suffering that comes with the quest for a "life well-lived." Happiness, con-strued in this manner, is not merely a fleeting burst of good and pleasurable feelings, but an attitude that is and can be sustained and nourished through intentional cultivation and practice.

14. Grawe, *Neuropsychotherapy*, 244.
15. Csikszentmihalyi, *Flow*, vii.

Interestingly, happiness as a "life well-lived" is more than just a philosophical statement. It is also an assertion backed by empirical studies on the science of happiness. This new twist on an age-old preoccupation is gaining much traction and shifting people's perspectives about it. According to the literature, this seemingly elusive yet reachable positive emotion contributes to favorable and positive outcomes on all domains of life, including a stronger immune system and longer life expectancy. Neuroscientists have also been able to map brain areas involved in the experience of happiness and pleasure, proving once again the intricate and synergistic interplay between mind and body. Our innate need for happiness, therefore, indicates our predisposition for growth and strivings to become better and flourishing human beings that not only benefits us, but also those around us.[16]

But happiness conceived in this manner still remains a formidable challenge, an elusive and illusory goal for many of our queer siblings. Even the very thing that usually provides meaning and anchor, that is, being able to participate fully in religious life, is taken away from them, or their sense of calling is dismissed or put into question. This cavernous gap or conflict between their intentions or personal goals (e.g., living authentically) and perception and experience of reality (e.g., homophobia) gets wider and deeper, driving them even further into untenable position. There is also intra-psychic wounding created by a conflation of painful experiences that makes them susceptible to all sorts of mental and relational difficulties. So, instead of experiencing positive emotions, they get flooded with negative cognitions and feelings that are metabolized and internalized, inducing pervasive feelings of shame, anger, judgment, and other similar affects. The incongruity between what one needs to survive and thrive and what is made permissible, available, and accessible to meet these needs by the larger social world is stark and causes so much distress, dis-ease, and despair. Consequently, one gets blamed or shamed or further ostracized for these apparent failures, which are usually deemed as self-induced or an outgrowth of one's flawed and weak nature.

It is disheartening indeed to realize, if we step back from this brief survey, the seemingly insurmountable challenges queer Christians face in meeting these basic human needs. I offer this to drive the point that we are no different from everyone else when it comes to what constitutes humanity and what facilitates human flourishing. We all are cut from the same

16. Kringelbach, "Neuroscience of Happiness and Pleasure."

cloth, so to speak, and therefore share the same human needs, as well as the pathways and opportunities for these needs to be met. Except these reservoirs of resources are reserved only for some; and we are considered undeserving of them.

Amidst all these obstacles, however, we still see divine eruptions and display of human resilience time and time again. Among us are our queer brothers and sisters who are simply unapologetic in who they are and in their quest for living a life well-lived. Many are already "living out loud" and are helping others find their way. Very queer, indeed. Creative and subversive, inspired and inspiring, they are relentless and tenacious in their intent to breakthrough walls and/or create open spaces so that what is intrinsically ours by virtue of our humanity can be rediscovered anew, where our basic human needs are met in a different, tangible, and unapologetic ways. In turn, when we invest in helping others fulfill these needs, we can catch a glimpse of what it means to truly feel beyond the "pleasure principle" and experience and inhabit what it feels to be run by a "life-giving principle," that is, embodying the generative presence of God in us so we can help reenergize and regenerate others. It truly is a gift that keeps on giving.

Before we continue on our next journey, let me reiterate the following points. There is no reason to apologize when you feel this longing for deep and abiding connection with someone who will honor, respect, and love you as you are. There is no reason to feel guilty for wanting to take control back of your life, your body, your erotic desires. There is no reason to be ashamed when you feel positive about yourself and empowered to pursue your life's goals. And there is no reason to feel sorry or embarrassed for wanting to seek happiness and meaning that fits and fulfills your heart's desire. Why? Because these psychological needs are intrinsic and essential to being human and their fulfillment support our well-being and flourishing. What is utterly regretful, inhumane, and ungodly is when these basic needs are withheld, hindered, and simply denied from us because of who we are and whom we love. There is also something else that is going on here that legitimizes these violations, a much more pernicious mechanism that we will be uncovering in the next chapter.

CHAPTER THREE

The Blame Game

PSYCHOLOGY OF SCAPEGOATING

PASSING BLAME ONTO SOMEONE as a way of avoiding personal responsibility or culpability is a frequent occurrence in my work with clients in therapeutic contexts. Too often, a "problem child," a "rebellious teenager," or the "black sheep" in the family heaps up blame for marital conflict or familial discord. By pointing fingers at the vulnerable and dependent offspring within the marital-familial hierarchy, an exit door is swung wide open, leaving behind a mess of emotional entanglements, unresolved conflicts, and enduring threat-based response patterns for the "weakest link" to clean up. As in most, if not all cases, this gets messier and locks everyone in a never-ending cycle of the "blame game," which bears fruits of further psychic and relational wounding and instability. The difficult, painful, but rewarding work of addressing the core issue or problem is sacrificed in the altar of scapegoating that offers momentary gains expressed in a false sense of familial unity.

Peering into the hidden dynamics of scapegoating, at least on a psychological level, reveal a "dual-motive model,"[1] which usually operate outside of one's awareness. This defensive and self-serving maneuvering induces a sense of stable perception of "personal moral value" as a way of

1. Rothschild, "Dual-Motive Model."

50

minimizing guilt over one's contribution and responsibility for a negative outcome.[2] In the case of the "problem child," for example, inordinate negative attention is placed on him or her—from staying up late with friends to unpredictable behaviors to adjustment challenges that come with this age group—as a way of thwarting an acknowledgment of their own culpability for the family breakdown. The child is sent to therapy, which doubles as a confirmation of their collective projection, and everyone feels good about themselves for doing something right to "fix the problem." And then the cycle of blame rears its ugly head, and this time either the same person is scapegoated again, or another family member is sacrificed on the altar of guilt purification. Related to this motive is the mechanism's efficacy in providing a sense of stable perception of "personal control"[3] in the midst of a weakening family structure. Everyone stands on shifting ground, and with it comes discomfort and dis-ease, unknowing, and the prospect of total collapse of the system. To assuage this, a scapegoat is enlisted as the bearer of misfortunes in the family, who offers a convenient explanation and acts as a dispenser of control for an otherwise layered and complicated scenario. In a sense, a scapegoat is a person actively "destabilized" so as to achieve familial "stability" so that everything goes back to "business as usual" again.

The momentary triumph and release that is wrought by sacrificing one on behalf of the many signals an evolved ontological and cultural artifact that is not only embedded in all human relations but operates *ad finitum*, whose life-negating consequences are a grievous offense to human worth, value, and dignity. It gets even more iniquitous and demonic (not in a supernatural sense) when the scapegoat mechanism is legitimized by co-opting the sacred and make it appear as a divine initiative.

In recent memory and on a much larger scale, we see that this same mechanism yields atrocious and horrifying outcomes in the scapegoating and subsequent extermination of six million European Jews in Nazi Germany, the mass slaughter of Tutsis in Rwanda, and the ongoing ethnic cleansing of Rohingya people in Myanmar. Each had been credited as sole culprits behind the economic collapse, social stress, and political instability that blanketed their nations, and consequently bore the brunt of the dominant group's "crimes against humanity." Right close to home, the continuing violence inflicted upon black and brown bodies, hate crimes against Muslims, and the portrayal of immigrants as criminals and rapists give

2. Rothschild, "Dual-Motive Model."
3. Rothschild, "Dual-Motive Model."

witness to the instinctual response to scapegoat a particular group, usually of minority status, to assuage collective guilt and fear of losing autonomy and to project an illusory image of brute strength, power, and control. And since the cycle of injurious behaviors humans do to each other seems unyielding and hard to break, one cannot help but wonder if the scapegoat mechanism is more than just a psychological and collective defense, but an anthropological reality—a feature of the human condition and, by extension, of human relating. And if so, are we stuck in this never-ending cycle of sacrificing others in the altar of self-preservation, or is there a way out of it? From where does help come from?

The religious undercurrent of the scapegoat mechanism finds its genesis in the Old Testament. In Leviticus 16, we read the pivotal role of the "goat of Azazel" in carrying all the sins of Israel upon itself on the day of Atonement. In a highly ritualized manner, the priest transfers the guilt of the Jewish people onto the escaping goat, which is then beaten, dispatched, and driven out into the wilderness. This highly choreographed but violent and bloody ceremony secured salvific efficacy for the community. This, of course, foreshadows the same mechanism deployed against Jesus, but not for the reason we normally think. The Old Testament account provides the genesis of scapegoating, while the Gospel account of the passion of Jesus serves to undo this very same mechanism and subsequently offers us a radical way of conducting our life together.

SCAPEGOATING AND MIMETIC DESIRE

The cross as a symbol of the undoing of the scapegoat mechanism is elucidated by the French literary critic, anthropologist, religious scholar, and philosopher René Girard. His acute description and revelatory analysis of the culture constructing and sustaining of the victimage mechanism[4] is connected to his ontological claim that human beings desire according to the desire of another. The finer details of his theory are not within the scope of this book; however, it is important to provide a compendium of his theory, particularly its religious and theological ramifications, and relate them to hidden dynamics of the scapegoating of the queer community.

According to Girard's interdividual psychology, human desire does not originate from within the agential and isolated subject independent from external influences or promptings. Instead, as mimetic individuals,

4. Girard, *Things Hidden*, 3.

our human desires, whether temporal, relational, ideological, even religious or spiritual in nature, are borne out of imitating the desires of another. The meaning of desire, in this context, differs from erotic desires I have discussed earlier, in that the latter is a complex combination of social, hormonal, physical and psychological factors that orient us towards a particular kind of person.

In Girard's own words, "man [sic] is the creature who does not know what to desire, and he turns to others in order to make up his mind. We desire what others desire because we imitate their desires."[5] In other words, we have no clue as to what we want for our lives, oblivious about what is worthy and valuable, and therefore rely on others to fill this existential void. This lack of being causes us to look elsewhere, and this becomes our passage into what may resemble a sense of self that is derivative of the imitation of others. As discussed in previous chapter, we are initiated into this dynamic imitative process during early childhood development, which also coincides with rapid growth in neural development and intense activation of mirror neurons that underlie and support our innate mimetic capacities.

Hence, our desires for specific brands or styles of clothing to preferred profiles of potential mates, from vocational interests to political membership, social causes we support, and religious affiliations are chosen for us by another who also is co-opted into this same process of intersubjective desiring by the social other. In his theological appropriation of Girard's mimetic theory, Alison states that "all of these things are received by us in patterns that are pre-shaped by the desires of others."[6] These ready-made patterns of desires are mediated by our models who reflect or mirror back to us who or what to desire, and in the process conferring upon these objects of desires a sense of worth, value, and significance.

Incipient in mimetic desire is the potential for violence. Since two or more people are desiring the same object, there ensues mimetic rivalry, with the other seen as an obstacle to the acquisition or possession of the desired object. In this reciprocal, contentious and rivalistic exchange of the intrinsic worth and value of the object recedes into the background, and what takes center stage is the removal of the obstacle-model by whatever means necessary. As Girard asserts, "violence is the process itself when two or more partners try to prevent one another from appropriating the object

5. Girard, "Generative Scapegoating," 122.
6. Alison, Jesus the Forgiving Victim, 29.

they all desire through physical or other means."[7] The single-minded intent and intensity to eliminate the rival spreads like a contagion, drawing people into this matrix of violence or "mimetic crisis"[8] that teeters into an all-out war against all, threatening to tear apart social cohesion and unity. To thwart this social collapse, a sinister plot is conjured up by these warring camps by pointing their collective fingers randomly onto someone, usually considered by them as a weakling or a social misfit, and making him or her responsible for the unfolding conflict. In other words, a scapegoating mechanism is activated, which is a convenient way of releasing and transferring guilt onto another and secures the collective unanimity against the chosen victim. What starts out as an all-against-all is transformed into all-against-one, punctuated by a cathartic resolution ending in peace. Of course, the peace that comes upon this newly reconstituted community is the offspring of violence and victimage mechanism "built upon lies about the guilt of the victim and the innocence of the community."[9] Hiding this truth in plain sight is reinforced further by divinizing the chosen victim scapegoat through the attribution of "double transference,"[10] where he or she is considered to be both the cause of the conflict, and therefore must be driven out and killed, and the cause of peace, since the victim's expulsion recalibrates their social standing, relation, and sense of unity.[11] In other words, the resolution of mimetic crisis mediated by the victim turns him or her into a divine figure, a god, who bears both the transgression of the community turned lynch mob and the transgression of making him or her the bearer of their sins.[12]

In an effort to ensure and forestall a repetition of mimetic contagion, prohibitions are instituted and rituals and myths are enacted and observed. But far more than just mitigating violence, this social regulatory device is meant to conceal sacred violence committed against an innocent victim, the account of which is told only by the victimizers themselves.[13] With these in place, the community is afforded with unrestricted resources to create, develop, sustain, and then regulate human communities while hiding

7. Williams, *Girard Reader*, 9.

8. Girard, *Things Hidden*, 287.

9. "What is Mimetic Theory," para. 8.

10. Hammerton-Kelly, *Sacred Violence*, 26.

11. Hammerton-Kelly, *Sacred Violence*, 26.

12. Hammerton-Kelly, *Sacred Violence*, 27.

13. Girard, *Things Hidden*, 28.

in plain sight the fact that the evolution of human culture is founded on controlling violence with violence.[14] Sadly, not much has changed. This social mechanism is still at work, with the "face" of the victim going through numerous iterations over time. Hence, we get this eerie and dreadful sense that somehow, we are still standing on a shaky ground that is threatened constantly by a lingering mimetic breakout. Again, from where does our help come from?

Religion? Perhaps! But let us not be quick to assume that it is the panacea for this intractable predicament. In fact, the converse is also true. Religion has been and is used to other-ize and inflict violence on various minority groups,[15] those considered to be falling outside and resisting, challenging, deconstructing established dogmas and prescribed practices. This gives credence to Girard's claim that religion is not a response to a divine lure, or the "experience of the a priori Sacred, understood as ontologically prior to the individual or society,"[16] as most of us tend to believe, but is given birth by society as a protective response against mimetic delirium through the institution of prohibitions, rituals, and myths. It is "the sum of human assumptions resulting from collective transferences focused on a reconciliatory victim at the conclusion of mimetic crisis,"[17] hence, "violence is the heart and secret soul of the Sacred."[18]

In contemporary forms of victimage mechanism, this is nowhere more evident than the scapegoating of the queer community by the Sacred. Before exploring this more fully, let me say up front that the religious violence exacted against our community transcends these influential religious institutions and is part of a larger and well-oiled machine that involves the "bureaucratic State, with its criminal code, police, professional groups, official knowledge, and social policies"[19] to regulate erotic desires and privilege hetero-cis-normativity. Simply, religion is in bed with the state, whose liaison gives birth to the continuing violence committed against those whom they consider have fallen from grace, from the true ideal of heterosexuality.

---

14. Girard, *Things Hidden*, 115.

15. See for example, Bailie, *Violence Unveiled*; Cobb, *God Hates Fags*; Teehan, *In the Name of God*; Juergensmeyer, *Terror in the Mind of God*.

16. Hammerton-Kelly, *Sacred Violence*, 28.

17. Girard, *Things Hidden*, 42.

18. Girard, *Violence and the Sacred*, 31.

19. Kinsman, *Regulation of Desire*, 62.

I will confine the discussion on the scapegoating of the queer community within the context of the evangelicalism, particularly a strand that subscribes to the following positions with regards to the issue of homosexuality.

1. (Biblical teaching) Lifelong, monogamous, heterosexual marriage is the only place for genital sexual expression. This was God's intention to creation, as outlined in Genesis and reaffirmed by Jesus. All references in Scripture to homosexual activity are negative, confirming that lifelong monogamous homosexual relationships are not biblically equivalent to heterosexual marriage.

2. (Implications for gay Christians) Gay Christians should commit themselves to a life of sexual abstinence, as homosexual genital sexual activity is sinful. (Some evangelicals would here hold out the hope of healing, leading to the possibility of a fulfilling heterosexual marriage.)

3. (Implications for all Christians) Christians are called to hate the sin and love the sinner; therefore, although homosexual genital sexual activity is condemned, gays themselves are to be loved and accepted. (Some evangelicals would here point to the need to take a stand against homophobia. Others would point to the need to challenge gay Christians who persist in sin out of love for them.)

4. (Implications for the church's public ministry) Given the above evaluation of homosexual activity, the church cannot bless the same-sex partnerships or otherwise suggest that it views them as equivalent to marriage. Likewise, it is inappropriate for those in positions of leadership in the church to enter into same-sex partnerships, as this would imply church approval of them.[20]

The above articulation is the normative discourse of homosexuality that we hear repeatedly around us. It is a familiar message I have heard constantly from the pulpit as part of a worshiping community during those formative years in the Philippines. This message lingered on, proclaimed and talked about with such great intensity, passion, and certainty when I moved to the United States for my seminary education, and later as a faculty member of Christian higher education in Canada. It is astounding to think of the power and reach of the Western evangelical mind with regards to the issue of homosexuality. It is undeniably transnational, with its pipelines of prescriptive religious beliefs and practices flowing into the cistern

20. Vasey-Suanders, *Scandals of Evangelicals and Homosexuality*, 68–69.

of individuals and faith communities as well as the larger society, here and beyond, organizing and structuring acceptable patterns of erotic desires.

The intransigent apologetic established by the more exclusivist strand of evangelicalism surrounding homosexuality and the subsequent deployment of the victimage mechanism towards the queer community is a direct consequence, not just of particular readings of certain biblical texts as discussed in chapter 2. There are also tectonic changes happening on the societal level, as well as the usual suspects in the realm of the personal— psychological defense to deflect culpability and disown psychic scarring. A highly secularized society that is imbued with modern and postmodern sensibilities is witness to the rapid downturn in church attendance and allegiance,[21] and religious life receding more and more into the background and relegated to the private sphere. The ascendency of (post)modernism also created the conditions for cultural pluralism to thrive, and for individuals to question familiar scripts and reconstruct their identities based on their lived experience. The public and private lives of individuals are also becoming more segregated.[22] And with these cultural shifts affecting all areas of life, evangelicalism tightens its grip on orthodoxy by "codifying spirituality into methodologies and systematic theologies,"[23] as a way of solidifying control and influence on the faithful (collective control through containment). Hypnotized by mimetic contagion, this conservative evangelical hegemony[24] has chosen to scapegoat homosexuality as an identity marker with a fixed and nonnegotiable stance that renders those with differing hermeneutics as other, outsider, odd and defective heterosexuals.

In certain respects, the issue of homosexuality acts as a religious totem with endowed powers to not only separate the wheat from chaff, but also to induce unqualified obedience to scriptural prohibitions. Conformity and compliance to these prohibitions are considered as authentic expressions of one's allegiance to the Sacred. Appealing to scriptural authority based on a singular interpretation of the clobber texts becomes the battle cry; the very source of establishing evangelical unity.[25] To firmly establish its fortress against the intrusion of the secular and modern world and to further demarcate and preserve its conservative theological inheritance, there arose a

---

21. Vasey-Suanders, *Scandals of Evangelicals and Homosexuality*, 40.

22. Vasey-Suanders, *Scandals of Evangelicals and Homosexuality*, 40.

23. Vasey-Suanders, *Scandals of Evangelicals and Homosexuality*, 73–99.

24. Vasey-Suanders, *Scandals of Evangelicals and Homosexuality*, 54.

25. Vasey-Suanders, *Scandals of Evangelicals and Homosexuality*, 94.

heightening of homophobic discourse in churches and public squares. The normative discourse around homosexuality centers around themes that engender further scapegoating of the queer community while simultaneously inducing a sense of peace and righteousness for doing "God's work" among its fierce adherents (collective moral high ground). Living out the so-called "gay lifestyle" is considered an outright and unabashed defiance to God, and is regarded as a threat to children, marriage, family life, health, and the moral fabric of society.[26] It is also considered as a failure to "orient oneself towards the ideal sexual objects . . . an affect that is readable as the failure to reproduce, and as a threat to the social ordering of life itself."[27] These declarations have become the intransigent "talking points" of an embattled community in search of its identity and location within the wider and rapidly changing modern world.

The usual suspects in the realm of the personal are, well, predictable and utilitarian, but not sustainable. And just like what one spiritual teacher said, "what you resist, persist."[28] As a tried and true psychological defense, the scapegoating of the queer community conveniently hides, deflects, and disowns one's personal foibles and frailties. By focusing on the "great sin of homosexuality," one becomes distracted or is hindered from looking deeper into and working through layers of personal woundedness. The struggles of alcohol abuse and drug addiction, pornography, extramarital affairs, domestic violence, child sexual abuse, and persistent feelings of anger, envy, shame, and insecurity are accorded with casual indifference, and concerted efforts are thrown into the othering of the queer community. By speaking to the unrighteousness of those with same-sex erotic desires, a sense of righteous indignation is shored up, covering a multitude of transgressions that have gone underground and undetected.

Armed with biblical assertions for the "right kind of (hetero)sexuality" and biblical justification for the condemnation of the "wrong kind of (homo)sexuality," an honest inquiry or introspection into one's own failings and weaknesses as a human being becomes an option and not a first recourse (Matt 7:5). This righteous anger is worn as a badge of honor that signifies fidelity to Scripture or is displayed as some sort of an adornment that hides the tattered psyche that is in need of grace and healing. When deep emotional wounds are merely covered or ignored in the name of some

26. Vasey-Suanders, *Scandals of Evangelicals and Homosexuality*, 87–89.

27. Ahmed, *Cultural Politics of Emotion*, 145.

28. Tolle, *New Earth*, 74.

greater cause or mission (e.g., theological and ethical purity in matters of sexuality) they fester and leak into all sorts of self-and-other destructive behaviors.

More so, by scapegoating the queer community the more outright or subtle forms of microaggressions occur. Various manifestations of abusive power by those in religious authority become a distant echo or are drowned out by the noise and vitriol speech directed at "self-avowed practicing homosexuals." Here, the "hierarchy of ungodliness" is in effect with homosexuality occupying the top spot, and often the only item on the list. This maneuvering continues to seize the minds and resources of many who think so highly of themselves because of their privileged position of heterosexuality. By uniting together, through the process of mimetic delirium, to fight against the perceived enemy of the church they relieve themselves of the responsibility to address personal and collective beliefs and practices that tear at the heart of what it means to live justly, love mercy, and walk humbly before God (Mic 6:8). Consequently, social hierarchy is unchanged and enforced, and personal demons either projected or dissociated. In other words, it is "business as usual," and all this is wrought by the victimage mechanism, which renders the queer community a convenient target for scapegoating.

THE SCULPTING OF SCAPEGOATING

The victimage mechanism deployed by the normative discourse on homosexuality runs deeper than most people realize. The automatic "double transference" response and the attendant and simultaneous feelings of disgust and peace evoked by the discourse is supported and mediated by the operation of the brain that has long been immersed and conditioned to respond in this manner. The underlying premise here is that our ways of being and relating to our inner and outer worlds—our behaviors, belief systems, emotions and modes of thinking—are all "functions of a fully embodied brain . . . and has an evolutionary history," and has evolved into a "collection of task-oriented and problem-solving mental tools."[29] These specialized, instinctual and ancestral tools or neural wirings are deeply sculpted into the brain and leave an indelible mark that continues to shape contemporary behavioral, affective, and cognitive patterns.

29. Teehan, *In the Name of God*, 2.

What then triggers the activation of neural circuitry of our evolved brain that thrust certain groups within the evangelical tradition to possess ideations and perform acts of cruelty and violence against the queer community? As a start, and it is worth repeating this point again, there is a strain of violence embedded in the deepest structure of religious imagination,[30] which "flows naturally from the moral logic inherent in many religious systems"[31] and is grounded in our evolved psychology. Moral imperatives or prohibitions like the ones outlined earlier regarding homosexuality, according to cognitive science are instinctual, intuitive and affective laden reactions to social interactions (i.e., mimetic crisis) that are given rational justifications (i.e., to achieve a sense of identity and unanimity through the victimage mechanism). With the queer community seen as a threat to their moral and spiritual well-being the normative discourse on homosexuality is deployed, defended, and sustained, which automatically triggers deep-seated cognitive, behavioral, and emotional brain mechanisms[32] and responses to their adherents.

Inherent in this discourse is the bifurcation of people into two stratified classes solely based on their sexuality: The in-group (heterosexual) who has distinguishable notions of order, goodness, and moral superiority, and the out-group (homosexual) who is deemed to have fallen from Sacred favor and grace because they have adopted the grievous patterns of this world. Simply, the queer community is otherized[33] and scapegoated, which renders them vulnerable to all sorts of cruelty and violence. To justify such horrific acts, they are blasted with the "essence trap"[34] that locates their sexual expression as reflections of a flawed nature, character, or essence. Consequently, they are pushed further away to a more psychological distance (e.g., barred from full participation in the religious life) into the hated outgroups,[35] and suffer profound bodily injury, or "moments which position queer subjects as failed in their failure to live up to"[36] the heterosexual norm.

30. Girard, *Violence and the Sacred*, 31.
31. Teehan, *In the Name of God*, 147.
32. Teehan, *In the Name of God*, 42.
33. Taylor, *Cruelty*, 8.
34. Taylor, *Cruelty*, 9.
35. Taylor, *Cruelty*, 149.
36. Ahmed, *Cultural Politics of Emotion*, 147.

> In Evangelical Christianity, the Bible is perfect. It is God's word
> and it must be adhered [to] strictly. So, there is this expectation set
> on you, this goal that is set that you have to live by these certain
> criteria. And if you don't do that you are not one of us, and if you
> are not one of us you are probably going to hell because we believe
> it's true . . . and what we believe is true.

These are words uttered by Darren Freeman with such sadness, the
pained look on his face captured quite vividly in the documentary film *Cure
for Love*. His youth is riddled with inner turmoil and debilitating fear as he
mightily struggled to reconcile his same-sex desires with his faith as an
evangelical Christian. Gripped by fear that he was going to hell because of
his sexuality, a message he repeatedly heard from the pulpit, Darren locked
and hid himself in the closet from disparaging eyes. This forced isolation
and the unremitting pronouncements of judgment and condemnation
threw him into the abyss of despair and loneliness.[37]

Such moral prohibitions gain their strength when delivered and heard
repeatedly, causing stronger synaptic connections and neural patterning in
the brain to occur.[38] According to brain studies, "this strengthening tends
to happen when the neurons they connect are repeatedly co-activated. This
may occur when one neuron triggers the second, or when other signals
trigger both at once."[39] These beliefs also gain a foothold when they fit nice-
ly with other neural patterns already in place, and come with "emotional
boosters to help carve their impression into the cortex."[40] One such emotion
is disgust. Stimuli considered as disgusting elicit an arresting combination
of physical and behavioral reaction—from changes in breathing and distinct facial expressions to nausea and vomiting.[41] These aversive reactions
are preprogrammed, involving the stomach, the vagus nerve, and the brain-
stem so as to allow for "early detection and avoidance of disgust-threats,"[42]
which includes moral offense, an irrevocable charge leveled against the
queer community. But more than that, disgust is not just about responding
to disgusting objects, "but the very designation of 'badness' as a quality we

37. Nolasco, *Compassionate Presence*, 32.
38. Taylor, *Cruelty*, 149.
39. Taylor, *Cruelty*, 149.
40. Taylor, *Cruelty*, 149.
41. Taylor, *Cruelty*, 131.
42. Kazen, *Emotions in Biblical Law*, 93.

assume is inherent in those objects."[43] How often have we heard the words "You are disgusting because you are bad." Far too often, I am sure!

Simply, the process of scapegoating, on a neuronal level, relies heavily on the repetition of the core message, such as those outlined earlier, and is often intensified by the accompanying emotion of disgust. Unbeknownst to many unsuspecting speakers and hearers of the message, this gets etched deeper and deeper into their brain networks, causing them to react instantaneously in a predictable manner. The threat system of the brain is aroused and activated, and a defensive or offensive posture is taken. Rigid lines are once again drawn, commitment to the in-group's moral code enforced, and the out-group scapegoated—all in the name of religion. Invoking the name of God justifies these acts and reframes them as expressions of deep allegiance to and love for the Sacred. The more disgusted the in-group feels towards the out-group, the greater the avoidance or elimination of the source of aversive reaction is assumed.[44] Further justification is also elicited when the out-group is made to appear more dangerous and threatening, labeling them as people who have wrong ideas and are plague-bearing organisms that ought to be eliminated for the sake of public health.[45]

The structured and systematized packaging about the sinfulness of homosexuality tends to favor left-brain mode processing—logical, linear, representational—which also dampens or softens connections with the social mechanisms of the brain.[46] It also gains momentum in achieving greater conformity and unanimity when the message proclaimed is uncomplicated, consistent, and decidedly simplistic and supportive of the personal and communal narrative and identity of their followers.[47] Repeated activation of this mode of processing caused by repetitive negative messaging yields a strengthening of synaptic connections in this part of the brain.[48] Consequently, since this conditioning happens over a period of time and is peppered with negative emotional subtext, a stronger impression is carved out or sculpted into the cortex.[49] In other words, the left hemisphere can be co-opted to serve the cause of victimage mechanism by rendering the queer

---

43. Ahmed, *Cultural Politics of Emotion*, 82.

44. Nolasco, *Compassionate Presence*, 27.

45. Taylor, *Cruelty*, 158.

46. McGilchrist, *Master and His Emmisary*, 57.

47. Taylor, *Cruelty*, 149.

48. Taylor, *Cruelty*, 149.

49. Taylor, *Cruelty*, 149.

community as threats that must be defended against, thereby procuring a sense of peace, order, and unanimity for their community. The more hearers strongly believe the message they receive from the pulpit, the more certain they can be that the message is true.[50] Mimetic contagion and the process of scapegoating relies heavily on this type of communication exchange and neuronal activation.[51]

The left-hemisphere bias also dampens the ability to form meaningful bonds with others. The empathy circuit responsible for sociality (a non-judgmental, sensitive, open, curious, and hospitable stance towards another person), which is largely a function of the right hemisphere, is turned off. Through empathy, minds meet and hearts commune in unity; it promotes pro-social behavior, reciprocity, and cooperation, which help facilitate the flourishing of human society. But all that is sacrificed on the altar of having the "right belief" as opposed to the pursuit of "doing rightly" to all.

The failure to make empathic connection makes scapegoating inevitable, especially in cases where the line between who is in and who is out has been clearly demarcated. The tie that can bind one to another is severed such that the pain and suffering displayed by those who are pushed aside and treated as outcasts is obscured. The in-group is indifferent and unaffected by the suffering of their counterpart, and are deaf to their cries of anguish and blind to their harrowing plight.[52]

The brain captures these behavioral responses in fine detail, as revealed through various functional magnetic resonance imaging studies. For example, "it is discovered that the out-group members—merely by virtue of who they are, and not anything they have done—reliably elicit within the in-group diminished perceptions of suffering of others, and fail to elicit equivalent physiological and affective responses . . . these dampened empathic responses are related to less helping."[53] Falling outside the mythical heterosexual norm of the in-group a tactic of avoidance, expulsion, and elimination is firmly entrenched in their collective psyche.

What recourse does the queer community have in response to the victimage mechanism that characterizes the normative discourse on homosexuality? How might we refrain from mimicking this same process of scapegoating and instead lean into a gentle whisper of invitation to discern

50. Taylor, *Cruelty*, 145.

51. Nolasco, *Compassionate Presence*, 36.

52. Nolasco, *Compassionate Presence*, 31.

53. Cikara et al, "Us and Them," 149–53.

a response befitting our identity as God's Beloved Queer? In the following pages, I propose a contemplative and positive mimetic approach that gazes mindfully upon the Triune God, who is for us and over against nothing or no one at all. This mutual gazing creates an attitude of spaciousness and hospitality that mirrors the kenotic example of Jesus Christ who draws in us a dynamic of "faith beyond resentment"[54] and into a life of flourishing and communion with others. What underlies this is the conviction that God has got nothing to do with this social mechanism and instead comes to us to subvert or decolonize problematic notions of order, goodness, and moral understanding. It is also borne out of a felt experience and a deep understanding of being held and loved as we are (materiality or embodiment as a source of this heartful knowledge) by God. This state of security and safety in the presence of God creates a sacred safe space that champions the inherent sacred of each queer person whose human flourishing hinges solely on being God's Beloved. The image of us sitting around the eucharistic table with Christ, the forgiving victim and host, who we imitate as a mediator or model of non-acquisitive desire, will serve as background and foreground so we can begin to live by his example of unconditional love.

54. Alison, *Faith Beyond Resentment*, ix.

CHAPTER FOUR

Imitatio Christi

SCAPEGOATING REVEALED AND BROKEN

RELIGION IS A DOUBLE-EDGED sword. It can serve as an armament against a mimetic outbreak through its prohibitions, rituals, and myths via the deployment of the victimage mechanism.[1] Or, it can also be a transgressive instrument to disrupt and break the cycle of scapegoating and carve alternative spaces marked by non-rivalry, gratuitous love, and the flourishing of all. Taking the road less traveled, I bid the queer community to "queer and query" with me what this subversive response looks like, given the legacy of scapegoating to which we all have been forcibly subjected. This theological and pastoral experiment is both strange (non-retaliatory) and familiar (the retrieval of the meaning of the word "evangel," or the good news) and will hopefully turn the normative discourse on homosexuality and its resistance on its head. Now, isn't that a *comme il faut* queer response from God's Beloved Queers?

Our first stop requires that we take a leap of faith. That is, amidst the dissonant sounds and vitriol speech about our humanity, we descend deeper into our hearts (or ascend into the heavens) and with ears of faith hear the gentle voice of God saying, "*You are my beloved child, with whom I take great delight*" (Matt 3:17; Psalm 139:14; emphasis added). For many,

1. Girard, *Things Hidden*, 42.

this may be difficult to hear given the onslaught of disparaging messages from the lips of those who claim to speak for God. For some, there still might be some lingering or residual negative cognitions able to drown out even that still small gentle voice that speaks to the contrary. I am fully aware of the struggles that come with trying to break through walls thickened by messages of hate. Yet, on the other hand, I encourage us to remember and know even just for a moment that these false narratives, as discussed in the previous chapter, are embedded within the mechanism of scapegoating that creates for others a false sense of security, stability, and unanimity in the face of eroding identity, cohesion, and unity.

With this realization, we crawl back from under the rubble left by the ruins of exclusion and sacred violence, and in faith anchor ourselves upon the chief cornerstone (Eph 2:20). This is the kind of faith that refuses to be crushed by the debris of this mechanism so as to be recreated by the very person who laid bare the true nature and intent of the human sacrificial system through his own crucifixion on the cross. Christ has accomplished this not by display of might or power, but in self-surrender and loving forgiveness. In other words, we need to go back to the cross as the inaugural site of the promised salvation, but not in the way we have always understood this sacred drama. Because this time, the meaning and significance of this passion narrative is made strange to us because God's story of salvation is freshly told from the perspective of the victim of scapegoating, Jesus Christ.[2] And while we listen to a retelling of this story, we may soon discover being in the inside of God's divine life, energy, and action in the world and therefore primed to flourish, as queer folks, in more ways than we can ever dare to imagine for ourselves (Eph 3:20).[3]

Let us start with the default story first and then provide a queer reading of that same narrative inspired by the work of James Alison, who mined the theological significance and implications of René Girard's Mimetic Theory. Essentially, this familiar story revolves around three distinct themes—creation, fall, and redemption—and it goes something like this: God created all there is, including humanity, and it was good. However, this *creation* is deemed not "good enough" for humans and, following a series of events, they fell. This *fall* constituted a grievous sin against the Creator and resulted in the distortion of the order of creation. Here lies the problem, that is, humanity could not restore what they have broken, and they are

2. Alison, *Knowing Jesus*, 36.
3. Alison, *Undergoing God*, 2–3.

now in desperate need of reparation. God, being full of goodness, mercy, and justice, provided the way for the *redemption* of humanity by sending God's Son into the world, whose divinity and humanity effect the necessary satisfaction that humanity's sin exacted. The story reaches its denouement with a promise: those who trust in Jesus Christ whom God the Father had sacrificed to Godself will be saved from their sins. And with the indwelling of the Holy Spirit, they are now able to live their lives according to the original order of creation and are guaranteed a place in heaven when they die.[4]

There are variations of emphasis to this familiar story, especially when theological analysis is supplied. But for many a Christian, the contours and meanings of the story remain unchanged, and the implications for daily life that are meted out are undoubtedly a moralistic one—good Christian behavior is privileged as the rightful response for the bloody sacrifice rendered on our behalf. In psychological parlance, this is called "emotional blackmail" expressed in the guilt-inducing words "Look what I did for you—and you still want me to suffer."[5] But a queer reading reveals a subtext rarely uncovered and proclaimed, a reading that will hopefully provide the queer community with an alternative pathway or response to the age-old but still operational social mechanism of scapegoating.

When we problematize this narrative (or atonement theory in theological jargon), we discover a rather peculiar and troubling image of God—a vengeful and violent God whose demands for retribution presupposes vengeance through violent means. Putting it bluntly, God requires "the abasement of the other in order to be satisfied, and the other loving the cruel will of his Father."[6] Such a perception is jarringly counter-intuitive to what we know deeply about the character of God—a loving and non-violent God. But this intimate knowing gets sidelined when the violent act is couched in the statement, "I did it all because I love you." Doesn't this also echo the same twisted logic leveled by individuals and faith communities who are impassioned to "straighten the gays" through various and often violent tactics (e.g., reparative or conversion therapy)?

As is stands, this traditional reading also trivializes the impact of the revelatory and transforming power of the resurrection of Jesus Christ, which lies at the very core of Christian faith. Alison writes, "it makes out that Jesus' resurrection did not reveal anything new at all. It merely accomplished

---

4. Alison, *On Being Liked*, 19.
5. Alison, *On Being Liked*, 25.
6. Alison, *On Being Liked*, 22.

a deal whereby someone who was remote and angry remained remote and angry but created an exception for those lucky enough to be covered with the blood of [his] son."[7] The centerpiece of the story remains to be the treatment of sin, and anyone who professes allegiance is tasked to comport oneself around this sacrificial act. The moralistic stance taken by the normative discourse in homosexuality gets its legitimacy from exactly this way of interpreting those events. That is, those who fall outside the Christianized heterosexual norm must subject themselves to its prescribed practices. Within this mindset, resurrection power is supplanted by legalism, which then becomes the focus of Christian discipleship for many. Alas, there is another way of recasting the story. The resurrection of Jesus "did reveal something which was new—not new to God, but new to us. Jesus revealed that God had and has nothing at all to do with violence, or death, or the order of this world. These are our problems and mask our conceptions of God, of law and order and so forth."[8]

In the true Girardian analytical frame, we discover that our understanding of the sacred is actually tied to violence turned on scapegoats, then projected to God.[9] Sacred violence is its name, and it is the subtext of the default story that is often concealed from purview of many. Yet, the transformative and revelatory power of the Christ event cannot be suppressed or tightly contained. It is bound to break through this coverup and reveal, once and for all, the deception of sacred violence. God has got nothing to do with this violence. Any justification of violence committed in the name of God does not come from the true God[10] for the "actual initiative to kill does not originate in God after all, but in human beings attacking one another."[11] It follows then that the scapegoating mechanism deployed against the queer community is not God-approved. The converse is actually a more accurate reflection of the true God. That is, "God loved us so much that God longs for us to be free from these things so as to live forever, with God and each other, starting now."[12] And the pathway to this new life as effected by the death and resurrection power of Jesus Christ includes patterning our desire after the desire of God in Christ. Imitatio Christi, or the

---

7. Alison, *On Being Liked*, 22.

8. Alison, *On Being Liked*, 23.

9. Grimsurd, "Scapegoating No More," 50.

10. Grimsurd, "Scapegoating No More," 50

11. Schwagger, *Must There be Scapegoats*, 66–67.

12. Schwagger, *Must There be Scapegoats*, 23.

imitation of Christ, is what will break the cycle of sacred violence. It is also what makes possible and actual the flourishing of all God's Beloved Queers. How this positive mimesis is nourished and accomplished and what exactly is the shape of this flourishing will be the subject of this chapter and the next.

To further our queer reading of the story and to help us begin to imagine what exactly we are to imitate in Christ is to go back to the "scene of the crime," so to speak, to a time when the Jewish liturgy of atonement is first observed. As we time travel from time immemorial to the Christ event on Good Friday, we get to hear a different version, a different voice, a different account from the point of view of the victim[13] spoken in liturgical form, as opposed to a theory of atonement.[14] (And just an aside, for most queers, watching drama unfold makes the most impact.) As we let our religious imagination run wild and vicariously participate in this liturgical drama, we may discover that there is something that is being done for, towards, or at us, that we are undergoing something of great cosmic and personal significance.[15] That is, we are ushered into a life-changing event by someone who is prior to us, another Other whose desire is only to affirm and not thwart, and grow and not stymied our unique personhood and its many possibilities, that the process of new creation and a new way of being together is released through the gratuitous love of the Forgiving Victim, Jesus Christ.[16]

So, let us time travel back to the very ancient Jewish liturgy in the first temple. Here, we witness

> the high priest would go into the Holy of Holies. Before the high priest went into the Holy of Holies, he would sacrifice a bull or a calf in expiation for his own sins. He would then go into the Holy of Holies, taking one of two goats—a goat which was the Lord, and a goat which was Azazel (the "devil"). He would take the first with him into the Holy of Holies and sacrifice it to the Lord; and with it he would sprinkle the Mercy Seat, and all that was in the First Temple, the throne on which were the Cherubim. This was a place that only the high priest was allowed to enter. Now the thing is that after expiating his own sins with the bull, he would then don the white robe, which was the robe of an angel. From that

---

13. Hammerton-Kelly, *Sacred Violence"* 38.

14. Alison, *Jesus the Forgiving Victim*, 234.

15. Alison, *Jesus the Forgiving Victim*, 234.

16. Alison, *Jesus the Forgiving Victim*, 234.

point he would cease to be a human being and would become the angel, one of whose names was "the Son of God." And, he would be able to put on "the Name," meaning "the name which could not be pronounced," the Name of God. With the Name contained in the phylacteries either on his forehead or wrapped around his arms, he would be able to go into the Holy of Holies. (Remember the phrase, "Blessed is he who comes in the name of the Lord?" This is a reference to the rite of atonement, the coming in of the high priest—one of the many references to the rite of atonement we get in the New Testament—and of which we are largely ignorant!) So, he becomes an angel; and one of the angel's titles is the "the son of God." He sacrifices the goat that is "the Lord," and sprinkles his blood about the place. Now the High Priest is in there, and we, standing outside, are full of curiosity, waiting to see him emerge, and watching for God's signs of God's interaction with him. There is the High Priest, in the Holy Place, with us outside, and he is being ministered to by angels, he is communing with the angels who were with the Lord at the beginning of creation. He is spending time in prayer, for it is during this period that he will expect to become interpenetrated by the Lord whom he is going to incarnate for the rest of the rite. So, he will pray to become one with God, and that God will become one with him, so that he can perform the sacrifice and glorify God by making God's people one. This is what At-one-ment is all about. And then the High Priest emerges. He comes through the seamless veil pushing through the entrance. This is what we would have been waiting for, for this the Lord coming into creation, entering into materiality. And immediately he appears. The one who is in principle invisible can now be seen. What has happened now is that the Lord has come into our midst, vested in tunic of the High Priest, so the Creator is in the court of the Temple, making the whole place redolent of glory. At this stage the High Priest will either hand out, or hand back, to other priests, portions of the lamb. The symbol of this is that he is giving portions of himself to them. So, the priests have their portions, and now the High Priest, ably helped, would start to sprinkle, probably with great whiplash movements, the blood of the lamb over various bits of the Temple Court, and so over us, who would have been waiting for this. We would want to be covered by the blood of the Lamb, want to be covered by the protective skein which the Lord is weaving for us. At this stage, probably, the High Priest will advance upon the other lamb or goat which was to stand in for Azazel, the demon. He would lay hands on the lamb or goat, thus transferring to it all the sins and transgressions of the people, and the beast would then be driven with sticks and staves outside the Temple precincts to the edge of the precipice. This is the lamb or goat that has become known in English as the scapegoat. After the driving out of the sheep that stood in for Azazel, the High Priest, now fully clothed in his robes and tiara, bearing the Name, and amidst great music and rejoicing, so as to bring this great rite to an end. The Lord had successfully come among his people to atone for their sins, set them free, and restore creation. And thus, the rite would be achieved.[17]

In its entirety, the symbolic meaning of the atonement ritual is undeniably an act of diffusive love. God, the protagonist and initiator, from outside of creation, is moving towards us earnestly, without hesitation or conditions. The first of these outward movements of diffusive love is of God incarnating Godself in the flesh of the high priest to perform a sacrifice for God's people for no other reason than to restore creation, and not to satisfy some bloodthirsty deity,[18] as some theories of atonement would have us believe. The second is the slaughtered lamb who is a stand-in for the priest, who then is a stand-in for God, whose blood is sprinkled all over the holy place offering Godself for the people in a priestly manner.[19] The third outward movement is when the high priest, again as a stand-in for God, pushes through the temple veil donned in a high priestly tunic with gold filament, as a symbol of the one who has come through from outside of creation and entered and dwelt among us.[20] The invisible is now made visible, making the whole of creation holy and glorious.

As part of God's creation, we are freed up from the futility of deflecting the glory of creation away from the Creator, usurping and making it about us, which often involves scapegoating others. In this restorative and creative rite, God comes into materiality to "ensnarl creation from within, to make everything new . . . to unleash its full potentialities, as it were, and make creation full."[21] This rite mediates the possibility for our flourishing and therefore to be icons of God as we are, reflecting God's immense wisdom and glory, and not to make idols of one another, which is a petri dish for neverending scapegoating and rivalries.

17. Alison, *Jesus the Forgiving Victim*, 241–54.
18. Alison, *Jesus the Forgiving Victim*, 239.
19. Alison, *Jesus the Forgiving Victim*, 244.
20. Alison, *Jesus the Forgiving Victim*, 250.
21. Alison, *Jesus the Forgiving Victim*, 243.

There is another aspect to this ritual that is often dimmed by the emphasis on sin-narrative and an angry deity that predominates atonement theories. When the rite depicts the movement of God, who is outside of creation, into our midst to offer atonement or forgiveness through the sprinkling of blood over all the people in the temple court, it also makes a claim that God's diffusive love is prior to any transgressive acts committed. The apostle Paul captures this quite profoundly when he says, "But God demonstrates his own love for us in this: while we were still sinners, Christ died for us" (Rom 5:8). All these acts are "derived from forgiveness, which massively precedes them and enables them to be understood as that which can be forgiven."[22] Such generosity breaks open our heart for contrition and in so doing calls into being who we are called to be and to become.

It is quite evident that this Jewish priestly rite has got nothing to do with appeasing the wrath of God through sacred violence and everything to do with God taking the initiative to break the cycle of violence. Atonement starts with God and ends not with God but with us as its beneficiaries, thereby constituting us as a people who are going through transformation "over time as part of a benign divine initiative towards us."[23] God's movement towards us, at us, and for us is all-out, not withholding anything, but in consummate and diffusive love offers Godself to us and then more—"[he] who did not spare his own Son, but gave him up for us all—how will he not also, along with him, graciously give us all things?" (Rom 8:32). In other words, love, not debt owed to God or the appeasement of divine anger, is the only motive that fuels and keeps aflame the transformative and salvific power of atonement. The Gospel of John puts it very clear for us: "For God so loved the world that [he] gave his one and only Son, that whoever believes in him shall not perish but have eternal life" (3:16).

With this as a backdrop, the events of the passion narrative can now be seen in a whole new light, revealing in a consistent manner a very loving, gracious, and merciful God. We witness God taking on human flesh in Jesus Christ (John 1:14), which not only mirrors but fulfills what the rite points towards. We also encounter Jesus Christ as the authentic high priest (Heb 2:17; 4:14) in the order of Melchizedek (Heb 7:13–17) who has come out from the holy place and offered himself as the atonement for our sins. The self-giving act of God in Jesus Christ is not a guilt-inducing device of divine appeasement, but a demonstration of God's non-retaliatory display

22. Alison, *Jesus the Forgiving Victim*, 244.

23. Alison, *Jesus the Forgiving Victim*, 253.

of unconditional favor and consummate love for all people. This is further elaborated by how the Gospel narratives have depicted Jesus' self-giving act as double referential. The crucifixion of Jesus is about "simultaneously both the sheep—the self-giving God—and the tortured and driven out victim as the rite is both fulfilled and brought to an end forever."[24] In Jesus Christ we see a "subversion from within of the ancient liturgy of atonement"[25] expressed in "substituting himself for a series of substitutions,"[26] so that the human sacrificial system can be brought to light for all to see and therefore bringing it to an end. To put it more bluntly,

> what we have with Jesus is an exact inversion of the sacrificial system: him going backwards and occupying the space so as to make it clear that this is simply murder. And it needn't be . . . a realization that what Jesus was doing was actually revealing the mendacious principle of the world. The ways human structure is kept going is by killing each other, convincing ourselves of our right to do it, and therefore building ourselves over and against our victims. By revealing it, depriving it of all power by seeing it as a lie: "your father was a liar and a murderer from the beginning." That is how the "prince"—or principle—of this world works.[27]

What is hidden in plain sight and usually given sacred status towards some religious ends, that is, our penchant to sacrifice others considered deviants and disturber of "norms," is now rendered not of God, but of this world. By taking the place of the customary scapegoat and therefore at the center of what the liturgy is concealing, namely human sacrifice, Christ makes it possible for us to begin to live our lives without sacrificing others.[28] This is the site where the liturgical and ethical implications of atonement meet, and through it we are called to be co-creators with God, participating with him in the ushering and expanding of the kingdom of God that is marked not with burnt offerings of religious piety or sacrifices that entail the victimization of others, but to "act justly, and to love mercy, and to walk humbly with your God" (Mic 6:8).

The cycle of sacred violence that is of nefarious origin and enslaves and blinds people from the truth to keep the legacy of the victimage mechanism

24. Alison, *Jesus the Forgiving Victim*, 253.

25. Alison, *Jesus the Forgiving Victim*, 253.

26. Alison, *Jesus the Forgiving Victim*, 253.

27. Alison, *Jesus the Forgiving Victim*, 253.

28. Alison, *Jesus the Forgiving Victim*, 253.

alive has now been finally disrupted and broken not by a will to power, but in God's gracious act of self-emptying (Phil 2:5–11). By breaking this cycle, we are also shown "something about ourselves in Jesus bringing together the liturgical and the ethical understanding of victimhood,"[29] freeing us from our tendency to get caught up in it.

Indeed, the great reversal has been accomplished in that for once, religion, which is used to sanction violence, can now be a wellspring of streams of living water to wash away the strain of violence so wedded with religion for so long. But how do we ensure that this stream of living water continues to flow and run through the veins of our communal and personal life, thus bearing much fruit? This is no easy task, and it requires a steady, mindful gaze towards Christ, whose kenotic example we are enjoined to imitate despite the temptation to resurrect the blame game for some higher lofty goals, even those dressed as religious.

A NEW CREATION

The new space that has been opened up for us when Jesus Christ occupied the place of shame calls for a new, strange, and unfamiliar way of being together. Thankfully, we are not left to our own devices, for we have been gifted with the Holy Spirit (Acts 2:38), who now lives in us (Rom 8:11), producing wisdom and revelation (Eph 1:17) to discern clearly the ways of the cross from the ways of the world. Since we have been crucified with Christ, we are no longer held in bondage by mimetic rivalry that often results in unanimity over and against one—a despised other—but Christ who lives in us is inducting us into a new way of life, which we live by faith in him who loved us and gave himself for us (Gal 2:20). Simply, the place of shame inhabited by Christ has also become the place where a new vision of humanity is inaugurated, an "alternative vision of what human beings could be or are meant to be."[30] This new creation has come: the old has gone, the new is here, right now in the concreteness of our lives (2 Cor 5:17).

We participate in the unfolding of the new creation first and foremost by redirecting our gaze from each other to Jesus Christ as the mediator or model of non-retaliatory, non-acquisitive, and nonviolent expression of consummate love. The mindful and contemplative gaze is critical as we embark on a totally strange way of being together, especially when it comes to

29. Alison, *Jesus the Forgiving Victim*, 253.
30. Adams, "Loving Mimesis," 277.

relating with those who scapegoated the queer community. At first glance, this strange and unfamiliar way of loving might be counterintuitive for us who have been forcibly pushed to occupy the place of shame because of our sexuality. In fact, this may even be seen as adversarial or antithetical to myriad strategies of active and radical resistance we have deployed to counteract the victimage mechanism that resulted in outcomes of great personal, social, and political import. So, let it be known at the outset that the imitation of Christ does not mean giving up agency, as that will only reify victim mentality, and therefore plunge us further into a never-ending cycle of violence. Nor will it ever be about patterning ourselves after the mob by rallying our own community over and against those who have scapegoated us by becoming their persecutors as expression of retaliation.

As imitators of Christ, we are to give up our "lack of will to appropriate subjectivity, desire, and agency as those made in the Image of God."[31] It is often the case that this empowered subjectivity is distorted by the unrelenting normative discourse on homosexuality. The internalization of such hateful speech and behaviors has become so toxic that it often leads to self-hate and debilitating shame, which then breeds more violence to self and/or others. By turning our eyes on Jesus, who looks back at us with such delight, regard, and love, we begin to shed off false images of ourselves and reclaim our favored and bestowed identity in Christ. The self that is hidden in Christ makes possible a self-affirming stance in the midst of any threats to return or inhabit "falsely constructed subjectivity, abject will, and captive agency"[32] we have been forced to occupy that secured for others a sense of unity, stability, belongingness, and moral goodness. This, of course, takes a lot of courage. The temptation to go back to that familiar victim-perpetuator binary space that locks all of us in an ongoing spiral of sacred violence can be irresistible and overwhelming at times. So, the challenge before us lies in reclaiming our subjectivity, our "internalized system of mental, symbolic, and linguistic representation"[33] or internal models or schemas of self, agential priority, and non-rivalrous desires that benefit or flourish not only us, but others as well.

Here, we go back to the kenotic example of Jesus Christ, who we imitate as a fruit of an inspired mimetic response. This positive mimesis involves not only internalizing but also participating in Christ's intentional

31. Adams, "Loving Mimesis," 289.
32. Adams, "Loving Mimesis," 288.
33. Collins, "Girard and Atonement," 140.

states or desires so that his will to love is intricately woven with our own desires.[34] It is important to know that this is not simply possessing Christ's desires and then making them our own, but "rather something we share in only so far as we remain connected to Christ and his body,"[35] for apart from him we can do nothing (John 15:5). In Pauline terms, our mimetic participation in the desires and visions of Christ for humanity is analogous to having the "mind of Christ," that is, to follow his example of kenosis or self-emptying, as described in Philippians 2. Paul's admonition is not just about having the right belief, but also about living rightly, that is, living in light of the pattern of Christ's cruciform love.[36] The cross as the site of the cruciform love exposes the futility and fatality of scapegoating and the initiation of radical hospitality and openness with self and others, a dynamic of loving mimesis.[37]

The kenotic hymn in Philippians 2 offers a rather descriptive, unsettling, yet liberating form of loving mimesis. Christ's incarnational initiative is at its core a paradigmatic example of utter dispossession—"who, being in very nature God, did not consider equality with God something to be used to his own advantage: rather, he made himself nothing by taking the very nature of a servant, being made in human likeness" (Phil 2:6). As a mediator of non-acquisitive desire, he refused to grasp tightly onto his nature or status or honor that is due his name. Instead, he gave up everything and made himself nothing so that we can have the fullness of life (John 10:10). Though often thwarted by mimetic rivalry, he became poor to enrich us with abundant gifts and fruits of the Spirit (1 Cor 12:1–11; Gal 5:22–23) so that when we practice hospitality, we do it gratuitously. He took the form of a slave so that we can be freed from scapegoating others (Rom 8:2).

But he went a step further. In verse 8 we find, "and being found in appearance as a man, he humbled himself by becoming obedient to death—even death on the cross!" Yes, he willingly subjected himself to experience the extreme form of humiliation by occupying the place of shame, not to appease God's vengeful intentions but to make plain our own "inter-human violence."[38] He accomplished this not to shame us or make us feel guilty for our crazymaking projections, but to grant us unqualified forgiveness so we

---

34. Collins, "Girard and Atonement," 141.

35. Collins, "Girard and Atonement," 141.

36. Flemming, *Philippians*, 112.

37. Adams, "Loving Mimesis," 295.

38. Grimsrud, "Scapegoating No More," 52.

can begin to live differently, to truly treat each other as image bearers of a loving, forgiving, and compassionate God. This new way of being together confirms our mimetic participation in the life of God. As we go deeper into this divine life by remaining connected to the vine (John 15:4), we gradually habituate Christ's own desires or subjectivity. His descent towards the "downward path of dishonor, suffering, and self-renouncing love"[39] is also his way of entering the depths of human vulnerability and, by extension, directly experiencing the very depth of our own brokenness, suffering, and alienation.

For many of us, Christ's identification with us maybe difficult to grasp. After all, we have been made to believe that our banishment from the circle of the godly is sanctioned by God and so, instead of experiencing accompaniment in times of despair, we have only known absence and abandonment. We have incurred so much anger, disbelief, bewilderment, incalculable pain, isolation, even trauma because the bonds, emotional connection, and spiritual ties we have worked so hard to establish and to possess by virtue of being human have been severed so effortlessly by those who we thought are a bastion of hospitality, inclusion, love, and belongingness. This is likened to a "love spurned"[40] that surfaces when something you hold close to your heart and is a part of your being, of loving and living, has been ripped out and then you get told that "you do not belong here." That this somehow has a divine backing makes this experience even more harrowing and damaging, to say the least. The effects of such a cruel and ungodly treatment is innumerable and often haunts the victims to no end.

There is no judgment made for a gamut of feelings evoked by the claim that Christ identifies with us in that familiar place of shame. None at all. Nor is this assertion being pushed or forced upon us. Whatever it is that we feel or think, Christ's decision to love us precedes all that. Even at our weakest or moments of unbelief, his forgiving heart and tender loving gaze remains unchanged. Why? Because God has no part in our banishment and instead comes to us to heal our fragmented selves, help us remember our sacred worth, restore our place in the kin-dom, and chose us to participate in the flourishing of all, even those who drove us out to be exiled from those close and dear to us.

Since God is not part of the established sacred order, and in fact came to dismantle it (Matt 12:21–17), we can reimagine Christ as someone who

39. Flemming, *Philippians*, 114.
40. Alison, *Faith Beyond Resentment*, 105.

is the one searching for those of us who have been exiled and scattered and as the Good Shepherd will feed and care for us.[41] And when our bruised and broken selves are found by him, even our resistance to be touched, soothed, and held will not be met by displeasure or disappointment, but with empathy, validation, comfort, overflowing desire, and focused intent to heal and restore us.

As we courageously step into this unfamiliar space of unconditional regard, unhurried and tentative though it may be, we can be assured of the Spirit's gentle presence, nudging, and wise counsel (John 14:26; 16:13) so that we can begin to inhabit an "imagination that is set free to perceive the emerging voice of God, the creator and holder in being, the love and gatherer of the weak, a voice far too quiet to be able to be heard in the midst of all that wrath of spurned love."[42] The journey that accompanies this renewed and inspired imagination may not be easy as it may evoked painful and unprocessed memories. Some of us may need ongoing spiritual and psychological support through counseling and spiritual direction, pathways that may assist in this process of healing and recovery. There are, however, spiritual practices that may not only supplement this personal work but can also sustain our desire to imitate the ways of Christ.

CONTEMPLATIVE GAZE

The Psalmist declares: "One thing I ask of the Lord, this is what I seek; that I may dwell in the house of the Lord, all the days of my life, to gaze upon the beauty of the Lord and to seek him in his temple" (27:4). In the midst of threats and attacks from his oppressors, the psalmist remains unperturbed and single-minded in his quest for deeper communion with God, to seek only after God's companionship, and to set his sights, not on revenge and retaliation, but on beholding the beauty of the Lord. His response is a refusal to mimic the rivalrous and violent desires of his oppressors who are caught up in the never-ending cycle of violence and victimization, and to pattern his desires after the victimless and violent negating desires of God.

A way to initiate and sustain a life of communion with God, which poises the ears of our heart to hear "the emerging voice of God, the creator and holder in being, the love and gatherer of the weak"[43] is through

41. Alison, *Faith Beyond Resentment*, 115.

42. Alison, *Faith Beyond Resentment*, 116.

43. Alison, *Faith Beyond Resentment*, 116.

the practice of contemplation. Contemplation, as a soul habit, refers to a particular way of loving, experiencing, and knowing God.[44] It is both a gift, a direct action infused within us and therefore not something we can conjure up through human efforts, and an acquired response by us through intentional and ongoing cultivation.[45] Simply, contemplation is a different kind of seeing, and since we are constantly being inducted into desiring what God desires, it helps direct our gaze differently, that is, by looking through the eyes of God. During this process of beholding, we learn how it is to be

> given our desire through the eyes of another. The other is Jesus, the Word of God. So, we are being taught to look at what is through the eyes of the One who reveals the mind of God. That is, to be possessed by the mind of God ourselves. By being taught to receive ourselves and all that is around us through the eye and desire of God, our self becomes an incarnation of that desire. In other words: we are being taught to be loving lookers at what is by the One who is calling into being and loving what is. We are being taught to see and delight in what is by the One whose delighting is what give it, and us, to be.[46]

Hence, when we fixed our eyes on Jesus, we only see liking and utter delight looking back at us. And since we look at ourselves through these eyes, we gradually discover ourselves in a different light, as if for the first time, as someone delightful and loveable just as we are, no matter where we are. This different sort of seeing requires ongoing cultivation and nourishment to help clear away the scales of lies, doubts, guilt, and shame that blind us from truly seeing our sacred worth. It also supplants our instinctual reaction to join the mimetic craze with an experiential knowing that God is not over against us and is in no way involved in sending us to the mob to be sacrificed. We can then detach ourselves from the notion of this mob mentality and rest in this deep knowing that God is always coming towards us, not as a punitive and rejecting deity, but as someone who desires for our own flourishing. With this in mind, we can then just relax in the presence of God, whose beauty and glory we behold.

As an experienced communion with the divine, the soul habit of contemplation also releases the creative force within us yielding fruits of a

44. Nolasco, *Contemplative Counselor*, 9.
45. Merton, *Inner Experience*, 57.
46. Alison, *On Being Liked*, 1–2.

transformed life that is fully awake and fully alive. This wakefulness is characterized by "self-forgetting attention, a humble receptiveness, a still and steady gazing, an intense concentration so that emotion, will, and thought are all fused and lost in God who embraces them all. Gradually, by a deeper and deeper process of self-merging, a communion is established between the seer and what is seen,"[47] between the mind of God and our own internal subjective worlds, effecting change within. Hence, we can discern better the voice that comes from the true Shepherd and those whose intention is to lead us astray and make sacrifices out of us.

Listening to and habituating Christ's subjectivity is supported by many forms of devotional practices. This includes a way of engaging the Scriptures in which one progresses from spiritual reading to meditation to contemplation, practices that hone not only our ability to hear the word of God, but to become doers of it as well. As a form of prayer, spiritual reading involves the use of Scripture passages that are read silently and slowly until they sink into and awaken the mind and heart, readying them to consent humbly to the inner and creative work of God.[48] Often, this devotional practice leads to meditation, a form of reflection that makes use of reason, imagination, memory, and affection[49] to draw out inspiration and implication of the word of God for daily life. Put differently, our desires are reoriented to mirror the desires of God every time we look deeply and mine the wisdom and counsel contained in these texts. Along the way, and with constant practice, we begin to descend into a state of contemplation marked by stillness and silence in the presence of the self-revealing God.[50] This nondiscursive form of prayer quiets all mental activities, especially those that cast doubt on our true identity, and exercises "naked faith, presence, and radical intimacy,"[51] which then predisposes us towards greater dependence on God for our transformation and sense of belongingness.

As a way of being, contemplation also quickens in us the desire to imitate Christ, to model our ways of being in the world after him who is also the perfect and complete image of the invisible God (2 Cor 3:18). His incarnation, life, death, and resurrection made it possible for us to dwell in communion with God, where our true self is unveiled—made in the image

47. Happold, *Mysticism*, 70.

48. Finley, *Awakening Call*, 21.

49. Finley, *Awakening Call*, 21.

50. Nolasco, *Contemplative Counselor*, 36.

51. Finley, *Awakening Call*, 22.

and likeness of God (Gen 1:27). When we behold the beauty and glory of the Lord, we see "who we truly are, who we always were, and this seeing helps us claim our deepest truths,"[52] that we truly are God's Beloved. Now, pause for a moment and lean into this truth. Let these words possess, infuse, and permeate every fiber of your being and simply relax with this experiential knowledge. This identity that is bestowed upon us draws us ever closer to the heart of God, and from there we discover "how wide and long and high and deep is the love of Christ" (Eph 3:18) for us. So long as we remain grafted into the vine, we bear fruits that others may simply enjoy and get nourishment from, especially by those who starve for the kind of love that does not involve sacrifice of any kind.

There is no denying, however, that following and imitating Christ is costly. In fact, it demands from us a ready disposition to follow the way of the cross,[53] a willingness to embrace without any hesitation "a sharing in Christ's suffering, becoming like him in his death" (Phil 3:10). In the words of Saint John of the Cross, "those who take the spiritual seriously should be persuaded that the road leading to God does not require many considerations, methods, or unusual or extraordinary experiences. . .but one thing is necessary—self-denial and self-surrender to suffering and annihilation for Christ's sake. All virtue is contained in this."[54] Saint John is acutely aware of how the sacred order operates, of its need to use a scapegoat, a victim, a sacrifice to satisfy its lust for self-assertion, group identity, and to establish peace. And the only way to subvert this is to have the same mind and attitude like Christ "who being the very nature of God did not consider equality with God something to be grasped, but made himself nothing, taking the very nature of a servant, being made in human likeness" (Phil 2:6–7).

When we find ourselves being dragged into the place of shame because we refuse to participate in the established sacred order that is built around a scapegoat, we need not lose heart. The spirit of Christ is with us, "the spirit of truth which undoes the sacred lie is there to empower us to put up with the hatred which is how the collapsing sacred is held together, and it is by our standing up that the new creation will be brought into being through us."[55] The practice of contemplation, with its focus on

52. Pierce, *We Walk the Path Together*, 97.
53. Nolasco, *Contemplative Counselor*, 39
54. Saint John of the Cross, *Ascent of Mount Carmel*, 55.
55. Alison, *On Being Liked*, 11.

mindful beholding of the face of Christ in stillness and adoration, cultivates this heightened awareness and dependence on the inner work of the Holy Spirit, our Advocate, Counselor, and Helper (John 14:26).

EUCHARISTIC LIFE

The Christian life is marked, among other things, by a communal gathering around the table, where Christ is both host-priest and sacrifice. It is our way of actively remembering by making present the significance of the crucifixion of Christ and the call that emanates from this place of shame that he occupied. It is also the site where death is conquered and defeated (1 Cor 15:55–57) and where a new vision for doing life together is inaugurated (John 17:21). I hope that these terms have taken on different meanings for us in light of the foregoing, and that this queer reading offers a mind-shifting view of the transgressive nature of this sacrament. More importantly, I hope that by reengaging with this familiar sacrament, we may begin to habituate a life that mirrors or imitates Christ, that is, transgressing or subverting any sacred order that is built around sacrificing others with the spirit of grace, truth, and love.

I would like to use several sections or movements contained in the liturgy as laid out in simplified version of the United Methodist's *A Service of Word and Table I*[56] as an entry point for queer reflections based on insights gained thus far. The liturgy, reminiscent of the liturgy of atonement discussed earlier, starts with a "gathering," of summoning the professing community and drawing their attention to the sacrifice that ends all sacrifice. The practice of contemplation, of turning our eyes on and attending mindfully to the desacralized liturgy, prepares our eyes and hearts to both see and feel the undoing from within of sacred violence by Jesus Christ, the Forgiving Victim, who lets himself be sacrificed by it.[57] In this contemplative seeing, we are led to discover being freed from our bondage to interhuman violence so we can live more humanly as bearers of God's image.

The celebrant addresses the gathered community with the words "*The grace of the Lord Jesus Christ be with you,*" first utterances that proclaim God's constant first moves towards humanity, of God offering forgiving love that precedes or antedates any violation or violence we have done to God and each other. The incarnation of God in Jesus Christ now symbolized in

56. *United Methodist Hymnal,* 6–11.

57. Alison, *On Being Liked,* 12.

the eucharistic elements of bread and cup (Rom 5:8) captures this prevenient grace, the coming to creation by someone outside of creation, made available to all, without conditions or hidden violent agenda. During this process of discovery, we also become witnesses of and are emboldened to participate in the ongoing work of creation and restoration with the risen Christ, which involves the flourishing of all, as opposed to ordering the sacred around victimization that the world leans into to establish stability and unanimity.

In response to God's gratuitous invitation of table fellowship, we make our first move in petitionary prayer, specifically around the "cleansing of the thoughts of our hearts" that is run by the rivalistic, acquisitive, and victim-making desires of this world. All these desires that are given to us by the social other God knows, for "*all hearts are open, all desires known, and no secrets are hidden.*" Yet, God is not offended by these and will respond by the illumination of the Holy Spirit so that we may begin to love and magnify God's holy name completely—body, mind, and soul—from where we are as we are. So even in the beginning stages of the liturgy we express consent to the undergoing of a divine initiative that is totally for us and with us and not over against us.

Our petition continues, yet at this time attention is focused on the heartful and mindful hearing of the Scriptures and the proclamation of the Word. In this posture of prayer and by the power of the Holy Spirit, we express that Christ himself will explain to us what is said in Scriptures concerning himself, just like what he did to the disciples on the road to Emmaus (Luke 24:13–35). This may involve unlearning violence-justifying "atonement theories" that project a wrathful deity and relearning what it means to be the recipients of God's favor as enacted and foreshadowed in the "atonement liturgy" in the first temple and now fully realized in Jesus Christ. When the caricature is dismantled through this process of unlearning and the true character of God is revealed, we too may hear the written and living Word with joy, resulting in an Emmaus-like encounter with the risen Christ. Knitted together by the experience of God's consummate and cruciform love that shuns no one and embraces everyone, we rise and proclaim in one voice the essentials of our faith in the Triune God that informs our way of being together as one body with many parts, forgiven and awaiting a life beyond the temporal and into eternal union with God.

What happens next is a more explicit invitation to join Christ in his table. Already immersed in the reality that God has preceded us and therefore has begun the process of restoration and renewal, we break open our heart and *"earnestly repent of our sin and seek to live in peace with one another."* When we take to heart the ethical dimension of the liturgy of the Eucharist, we discover soon enough our own personal sin of complicity in the old sacred story of sacred violence. Acknowledging that there have been times when we have secured ourselves a sense of belongingness and security by sacrificing, victimizing, and demonizing a social other, a perceived rival, and that we are in competition for such prized social goods as reputation, respectability, admiration, acceptance, social standing, moral goodness, and unanimity, among others, is already a sign of a "heart-close-to-cracking."[58] As this heart continues to crack open, we also begin to realize that at times we have conveniently adopted the "position of victims, who make of positions of authentic marginalization sure platforms for protest for revindication of innocence and of sacred status . . . of pointing the finger at those who do not conform, demanding the sacrifice of those who do not participate in the unanimity of the group."[59] In other words, we too have been deeply influenced by and participated in the social mechanism of exclusion so as to make ourselves feel and look good, and our retaliatory measures we consider fully justified. When we renounce and confess our complicity in the "sacred forms of the past, with all their violence and their victims,"[60] then and then only we can truly seek to live in peace with one another. And right there before us at the center of the desacralized liturgy of the Eucharist is the site where these new forms of being and relating to one another emerge. Deeply convicted by the revelatory power of the cross in helping us confront our own violence and then be released from its hold, we then make our prayer of confession, receive Christ's forgiveness, and pass on the peace of Christ one to another in a deeply personal and meaningful way.

The core feature of the liturgy, which makes use of stuff from the earth to symbolize something of great spiritual significance, takes center stage this time around. In a highly choreographed and visible fashion, the celebrant lifts the bread and then the cup while motioning the actions and words of Jesus Christ (Matt 26:17–30; Mark 14:12–26; Luke 22:7–39; John 13:1—17:26).

---

58. Alison, *Faith Beyond Resentment*, 34.

59. Alison, *Faith Beyond Resentment*, 35.

60. Alison, *Faith Beyond Resentment*, 34.

Jesus took bread, and when he had given thanks, he broke it and gave it to his disciples, saying "Take and eat; this is my body." Then he took a cup, and when he had given thanks, he gave it to them, saying, "Drink from it, all of you. This is my blood of the covenant, which is poured out for many for the forgiveness of sins."

The liturgy makes present again and again God entering into materiality in human form, making visible through Jesus Christ what is invisible. The coming of God from outside creation to dwell among us in human flesh, "to make everything new . . . to unleash its full potentialities, as it were, and make creation full,"[61] is what salvation is about. It is never about getting a passage into some higher and distant place we call heaven, but about the in-breaking of God's creativity in the particularities of our lives to make it full and abundant. In another sense, the liturgy points to a disposition that deconstructs the old and worldly ways of gathering around the victim in the name of a false god to make us all look good, and it reconstructs a new vision for humanity as exemplified by Christ, who sacrificed himself to end all sacrifices. The elements of the bread and the wine, a stand-in for the body of Christ broken for the world and blood spilled for the forgiveness of our sins, are broken symbols to make concrete and actual God's self-giving love so that, in receiving them, we signify our desire to have the mind of Christ, to be like Christ. And by sharing in one loaf and drinking from the same cup, we join the communion of saints at all times in all places in all levels of social, economic, and political life[62] (Matt 5:23–24; 1 Cor 10:16–17; 1 Cor 11:20–22; Gal 3:8) to promote "justice, truth, and unity" as well as "human personality and dignity."[63] For the one catholic and apostolic church to accomplish this, it must break away from any sacred order that is established around the victimage mechanism and be "broken" itself in order to serve others in self-emptying and compassionate love.

The apostle Paul understood this completely when he placed the celebratory meal within the context of the church at Corinth that is beset by disunity and betrayal, like the church of today. The symbolic meaning of the Lord's Supper has eluded the church, and their divisive and selfish behaviors have rendered them "guilty of profaning the body and blood of the Lord" (1 Cor 11:27). For instead of breaking bread together as one body of Christ, they allowed themselves to be ruled by rivalrous and exclusionary

61. Alison, *Forgiving Victim*, 241.

62. Nolasco, *Compassionate Presence*, 19.

63. *Baptism, Eucharist and Ministry*, 11, 12.

sensibilities and, lacking in compassion, neglected and pushed aside the poor amongst them. Simply, they chose to be run by the old sacred script of erecting divisions so as to establish a strong demarcation between the good and the bad, between those with established sense of moral uprightness and those who have fallen into disrepute. Sacred violence has once again ruled in their midst. But Paul issues a challenge by helping them remember, through the Lord's Supper, how this has already been exposed and dismantled by the atoning work of Christ on the cross.

Summarily, the celebration of the Eucharist is an ongoing invitation for us to participate in the ministry of reconciliation (2 Cor 5:18), to reflect in our life together the spirit of sharing and unity in Christ, and to subvert any attempts at sacrificing others in the altar of sacred violence. For queer Christians, the Eucharist is also a space for a heart close to cracking, a space where we begin to understand that God has got nothing to do with the violence inflicted upon us because we are gay. As an expression of solidarity with those victimized by this sacred order, he occupied that place of shame to finally reveal its human origins and transform that very same place into a space where new life can begin.

With Christ present as the "crucified one, and we as penitents learning to step out of solidarity with our multiple and varied modes of complicity in crucifixion,"[64] we come to the table set before us by our host and model with thanksgiving and perhaps a little giddy to claim our place as "co-participators in an unimagined creation."[65] Yes, you and I have been lifted from this place of shame and are now called into being by God, who really likes and takes delights in us as we are. Perhaps God is a little giddy as well to see who we could be and might become as recipients of this vivacious and creative force at work in us and all of creation. So, we take all that with us, and we lean into the experience of being summoned into an intimate table fellowship with God and make use of it as our own bread and wine as we pattern our desires after the eucharistic life similar to that of Jesus Christ, our model and mediator of God's own victimless desires.

RADICAL COMPASSION

The parable of the Good Samaritan in Luke 10:25–37 offers us another window into a life transformed by the imitation of Christ. A queer reading

64. Alison, *Faith Beyond Resentment*, 34.

65. Alison, *Faith Beyond Resentment*, 123.

of this very familiar text situates ourselves not as the man who was robbed and was left for dead on the street (v. 31), but as the protagonist in the story—the Good Samaritan—who showed compassionate love towards this wounded man and exposed the incongruity between religious belief and action. This is not to ignore the plight of many of our wounded queer siblings, brothers, and sisters in the Lord who are still victims of the social and spiritual mechanism of exclusion. Far from it. Nor is the reading about posing judgment towards the priest and the Levite who looked the other way. The role reversal advanced here is meant to highlight our active participation in creating redemptive spaces that shun no one but encircle everyone. We respond to this call to be cocreators with God right from our redeemed experience of exclusion by the social other and our radical inclusion secured for us by another Other—God.

Always transcending the limits and often divisive nature of human categories, Jesus' use of the Good Samaritan[66] to be an exemplar of compassionate love parallels God's call for us to embody "neighborly love that is scandalous in its inclusivity, outrageous in its display of concern, and radical in its generosity."[67] We start this incarnational ministry of loving mimesis right where we are, wherever that may be. This may mean working with our allies to rebuild our own faith communities who have been co-opted by the larger and social realm of principalities and powers (Eph. 6:12) that operate around and is sustained by the mechanism of exclusion. We pattern our response after the example of Jesus, who took the temple system to account because it had unchained itself from its religious purpose and challenged its entanglements with the economic and political power of their time (Mark 11). We call into question and subvert the practice of "institutionalism" where the priority is placed on survival, order, security, and peace[68] and to recapture what it means for the church to become God's instantiation here on earth, through our radical hospitality and scandalous inclusivity.

Our faith communities also need our outrageous display of concern as they are also bleeding out and losing vitality to be witnesses to God's action in the world because of these tribal wars. Like the wounded man in the parable, our churches need our engaged compassion so that, along with others, we can provide an empathic and caring presence and sharing of

66. See also Scanzoni and Mollenkott, *Is the Homosexual My Neighbor?*
67. Nolasco, *Compassionate Presence*, 45.
68. Grimsrud, *Violence Renounced*, 56.

resources to help in the restoration of the body of Christ (Luke 10:33–35). I know that it is easier sometimes to just walk away (and some have) so we can protect ourselves from the never-ending cycle of scapegoating or heal from the trauma that this mechanism has inflicted on us. I consider this to be a wise and healthy decision, as taking refuge is also a necessity, not only for our immediate benefit, but also for the work of restoration that beckons us. This restoration comes in the form of mediating the presence of God in the midst of all the brokenness we see in our faith communities, even if we get rejected once more. As we are no longer run by a pattern of desire that seeks to engage us in the perpetual game of sacred violence, we can stand firm and remain steadfast in God's call to love our enemies (Matt 5:44–45). Put another way, for loving mimesis to be a true reflection of Christ's cruciform love, we must also take into account the liberation of those who have persecuted us and benefited from the exclusionary mechanism by showing the love, because God does.

Jesus' call to love our enemies is a symptom, a derivative, an offshoot of being grafted into the vine, of being children of God who causes the sun to rise on the evil and on the good and sends rain on the righteous and the unrighteous (Matt 5:45). In the eyes of the world, only a few merit the favor of God, and they are usually determined by the ones in power who wield "selective grading of human beings and severe penalties inflicted for its rejection."[69] But in the eyes of God we all are equal recipients of mercy and love. No one is given privilege because everyone is heirs to God's generosity. Thus, "to say that God does not sit atop the pyramid of power legitimating the entire edifice, does not favor some and reject others, is to expose the entire structure as a human contrivance established in defiance of God's very nature."[70]

The call to love evenhandedly does not only call out our shared beginning and parentage under God, but it also makes us acutely aware of our own complicity in living in enmity with God.[71] Through an inspired and graced humility brought by the renewing power of the Holy Spirit, we come face to face with the reality that we, too, are a mixture of just and unjust, of good and evil, that we have participated in the social mechanism of exclusion, perhaps not when it comes to the issue of homosexuality, but in other forms of inner violence not seen through the naked eye. Hence,

69. Wink, *Engaging the Powers*, 267.

70. Wink, *Engaging the Powers*, 267.

71. Wink, *Engaging the Powers*, 267.

like everyone else, we too are in need of God's forgiveness, which God has lavishly offered to us long before we have come to our senses (Rom 5:7–8). This gift that keeps on giving has "reached us first, re-imagining it as something done for us and coming to meet us, and as it meets us, enabling us to be turned into imitators"[72] of Christ so we can extend that same gift to others, friends and foe alike. In other words, God has come to us with unconditional expression of compassionate love and forgiveness, and is renewing our very being daily so as to bear the fruit of love (1 Cor 13:1–3) that embraces all, including those who have put us in the place of shame.

In this regard, the call to love our oppressors or victimizers is pastoral, that is, to help them recover their true humanity."[73] The mimetic contagion that usurped their agency, creativity, and regard for other fellow human beings has turned them to become active participants in the deployment of sacred violence. This mechanism is far greater and more insidious than merely subscribing to group-constituting discourse. It is institutionalized beyond the church walls and has the backing of the "bureaucratic State, with its criminal code, police, professional groups, official knowledge, and social policies."[74] By responding in compassionate love marked by empathy towards their condition and forgiveness as we have been forgiven, we all have a chance at becoming what God has created us to be and to have a "spirit of generosity that is willing to submit to outrages and injustice, not in a cowardly fear of retaliation, but in order, if possible, to awaken God in the other's soul."[75] The awakening of God in each other entails that we see past the façade constructed by the social other and acknowledge and connect with the divine image in all of us, the source of our humanity.

The inspiration and progress to imitate Christ is sustained by the practice of prayer, whatever form this may take. In this context, prayer is dispositional, a way of expressing our utter dependence on God, who liberates us from our interior battles and strengthens us in engaging these principalities and powers in a non-retaliatory and non-victimizing manner. It is our primary shield, our first recourse so that the hypnotizing nature of mimetic contagion that seizes our imagination can be broken, and our imitative capacities are redirected and drawn to Christ, our model and mediator. For this reason, it is important that we attend faithfully to our

72. Alison, *On Being Liked*, 38.

73. Alison, *On Being Liked*, 276.

74. Kinsman, *Regulation of Desire*, 62.

75. Wink, *Engaging the Powers*, 276.

prayer life as this "may be the interior battlefield where the decisive victory is first won, before engagement in the outer world is even attempted."[76] It is possible that we will be triggered, that our efforts to pursue justice will be mightily thwarted by the social other, that our resolve will sometimes crack, and our energy be zapped by the enormity of the task. Prayer is our lifeline, the unbreakable conduit to God who is the source, the sustainer, and our ever-present support. And so long as we are deeply planted in the interior garden of our soul, bathed in prayer, we will remain steady, awake, and alert amidst the challenge that comes with our participation in God's creative and redemptive work.

Prayer also keeps us protected from getting lured into new forms of activism that are characterized by willful assertion bordering towards "self-justifying good works" that may entangle us back to the perilous game of scapegoating. Because of our mimetic nature, it is easy to mirror back other forms of activism because of our shared affinity and commitment in pursuing justice. Our starting point, however, is different in that this justice-making is an outworking of our affinity, not with the cause per se, but with God, who is the ultimate bondage breaker. Prayer, therefore, keeps us in sync with God, neither forging ahead nor lagging behind, but in willing submission and dependence to God.

Lastly, prayer keeps us real. That is, it is God "rather than ourselves who initiates prayer . . . we are always preceded in intercession. God is always already praying within us. When we turn to prayer, it is already the second step of prayer."[77] Our act of praying is a response to the prevenient grace at work within us, meant not to change God but to change us (Rom 8:26–27). Part of this inner work that prayer does within us is not to "do everything, to heal everything, to change everything,"[78] but to discern clearly and humbly the shape of our divine calling, starting from where we are with what we have.

76. Wink, *Engaging the Powers*, 297.

77. Wink, *Engaging the Powers*, 304.

78. Wink, *Engaging the Powers*, 307.

CHAPTER FIVE

Flourishing the Beloved

As BELOVED HEIRS OF God, we too are meant to flourish. It is part of our creatureliness, a marker of what it means to be fully human. On a fundamental level, human flourishing means living a life where basic human needs are met, both physical and psychological. From there, the flourishing evolves into the pursuit of loving God and loving neighbors as we love ourselves (Luke 10:27). Though the shape of our flourishing is varied, there lies a shared or common experience of emotional stability and resiliency, vitality and engagement, and positive relationships, and of being committed to or invested in championing the flourishing or well-being of others in all ways possible. Desiring the flourishing of all mirrors or imitates God's heartfelt desire for all of creation, for God has come so that we may have life and have it to the full (John 10:10). Hence, the fullness of our creation, of truly becoming the person we are created to be, is contingent on God, for apart from this divine initiative we can do nothing.

I know that it is often difficult to imagine that God desires our flourishing. At times, it is even harder to believe that we even deserve to flourish. If we do, what is made available to us is that we have to be a person other than our true selves to partake of it. In other words, we are barred from or are considered as undeserving recipients of God's generosity because of our sexuality, at least according to the purveyors of the victimage mechanism who are the architects of the sacred violence inflicted upon us.

I hope, though, that by now, through the preceding discussion, we can boldly say that this social mechanism is a gross distortion of God's character and a gross violation of our inherent dignity as bearers of divine image. God as love only desires the flourishing of the beloved—and that includes you and me and the rest of the queer community. We do not have to be someone other than ourselves to merit such favor. God's gratuitous love and intentions extend and include us and start from where we are. From that unique circumstance, God will begin to fashion us to be the sort of persons we are meant to be—as lovers of God and lovers of all—without displacing our queerness. For there is no other place that God would rather be to display God's manifold works than to be in each of us. We are, after all, God's masterpiece and God's beloved queers.

Having said that, I am also keenly aware that the tide is strongly set against us, and that the "larger household of reality"[1] remains inhospitable towards us. Yet, in the absence of such fit, between how the world is constituted and what it means for human beings to flourish, we remain hopeful that "that the presence and activity of the God of love, who can make us love our neighbors as ourselves, is our hope and the hope of the world—that the God is the secret of our flourishing as persons, cultures, and interdependent inhabitances of a single globe."[2] And God who started this marvelous work in us, who entered into the concreteness and vicissitudes of our lives, will continue the work of redemption, reconciliation, and restoration until it is finally finished on the day when Jesus Christ returns. While we participate in God's restorative act and while we eagerly await the dawn of the fullness of creation, there are specific and practical soul habits that, when nourished and cultivated, will support our flourishing, especially in the midst of a culture that is still run by the social mechanism of exclusion. We now turn to these spiritual habits for the queer soul.

First, breathe deeply, slowly, and gently. This may appear quite odd to you, and perhaps you might wonder what the connection is between breathing and the cultivation of an awakened awareness of God's ongoing interior work in us. Like most people, we are often unaware of the rhythmic pattern of inhalation (breathing in) and exhalation (breathing out) that carries us through our daily lives; animating and anchoring our very being. It is automatic, unconscious, and mostly involuntary. However, we do have

1. Volf, "Human Flourishing," 24.
2. Volf, "Human Flourishing," 24.

some capacity to influence the pace of our breathing, especially in the midst of disquieting situations.

The emotional stress induced by the ceaseless barrage of homophobia tends to intensify such feelings as anger, fear, sadness, and shame, and can significantly alter the inner workings of our sympathetic nervous system to a level that is detrimental to our physical and psychological well-being. The body's alarm system goes into high gear and never lets up, especially when exposed repeatedly to traumatizing events. Hence, we find ourselves constantly on high alert, disquieted, tense, and afraid. Our body gets flooded with cortisol, a stress hormone, resulting in various physical ailments (e.g., increased blood pressure, compromised immune system) and psychological maladies (e.g., depression, anxiety, substance abuse).

Slow, deep, and gentle breathing can quiet down a dominant and overactive sympathetic nervous system. By voluntarily choosing to take a few deep abdominal breaths, our parasympathetic nervous system gets activated, relaxing our muscles and slowing our heart rate, therefore producing a state of calm and clarity.[3]

As a start, carve out a time during the day and spend at least five minutes (at six breaths per minute) practicing diaphragmatic breathing until it becomes familiar and natural. Once you feel comfortable, pair the word "love/like" during inhalation and breathe out the word "loved/liked" in exhalation. By pairing the physical act of breathing with emotive, evocative, and positive words, you enhance your capacity to stay grounded and strongly anchored by love that drives out fear and make actual this new being who God is calling forth within you.

There will be times when you will be co-opted again to play the role of the scapegoat as a veiled attempt of others to hide their internal crisis or shore up unanimity. They will try to project their own fears and insecurities onto you and exact approval, group belongingness, and sense of goodness by mimicking, approving, and sanctioning acts of cruelty towards you.

When this happens, remember to pause and breathe mindfully so as to create a space within your mind and heart so that you can respond not as a rival on a defense (or offense), nor as a victim acquiescing to the patterns of their desires, but as a forgiven follower of Christ whose Spirit enables you to remain unanxious and nonreactive, disentangled from the shackles of the scapegoat mechanism. Remember that the "the spirit of truth which undoes the sacred lie is there to empower us to put up with the hatred

3. Siegel, *Mindful Brain*, 31.

which is how the collapsing sacred is held together, and it is by our standing up that the new creation will be brought into being through us."[4]

There is another dimension to breathing that I find rather compelling, which I hope will evoke sustained interest regarding its manifold benefits and significance. When vocalizing the word YHWH, the name ascribed to God, one hears the soft sound of breathing.[5] Try to pronounce the letters "Yod-Hei-Vav-Hei" for YHWH and see if it resembles the sound that you make when breathing. Think of the breath that we take in, the air that animates our being and makes us alive (Acts 17:28), as a proclamation and reception of God, who is the source of all life (Gen 2:7). The enlivening presence of God is made immediate by every breath we take, and the intimacy and transcendence it signifies points to our origin and utter dependence on the Breath of Life. So, when you are feeling "out of breath, out of sync, and out of place" for whatever reason, remember to breathe gently, slowly, and deeply, and let yourself be bathed in the experiential knowledge and awareness of the presence of God in you who loves, likes, and delights in you.

Second, pursue an attitude of equanimity. By this, I mean seeking and maintaining a calm, balanced, or even-mindedness in the sea of emotional negative valence and mimetic contagion that often accompanies the normative gay discourse. The unwelcoming and intolerant attitude displayed, and the damaging and vitriolic narrative spoken by others, is the seedbed of resentment, anger, anxiety, depression, and shame. These unpleasant and often debilitating emotions become our insulation protecting us from further threats or attacks. Anger and resentment make us feel empowered, anxiety distracts us from recognizing our deep hurts, depression slows down the chaos around us, and shame makes us disappear into "no-one-ness." Sadly, with constant exposure to such painful and traumatizing experiences, this repertoire of responses become automatic, instinctual, and repetitive, leaving traces of deep wounding that never seems to heal. We get caught up in this mimetic cycle and find ourselves enslaved by the very reactions that once provided relief and refuge. Equanimity offers a way out of this captivity into greater emotional freedom and behavioral flexibility[6].

4. Alison, *On Being Liked*, 11.

5. Audlin, *Gospel of John*.

6. Desbordes, "Moving beyond Mindfulness," 356–72.

Nurturing a calm, stable, and unperturbed disposition also targets our tendency to perpetuate and prolong pleasant and rewarding experiences to the point of getting addicted to them. The rush of "feel-good" moments associated with adventurous or risky behaviors often act as an analgesic to counter the ache buried deep within. The suffering that comes with being gay is often so overwhelming that we get enamored by experiences that provide relief and respite. This instinctual human drive to minimize pain and heighten pleasure sometimes sets off a cascade of behaviors that captivate and excite our imagination and propel us into obsessive pursuits of these pleasurable experiences. Once engulfed by their gratifying and numbing effects, we hunger for more of the same and find ourselves getting lost in them. Equanimity creates an alternative stance towards our propensity to grasp firmly onto what makes us feel good (or powerful by holding onto anger or resentment), not by dismissing them but welcoming them without getting attached to them.

Now, it is easy to conflate the notion of equanimity with indifference. But contrary to what most people think, the former is qualitatively different from the latter. Being equanimous means being open and attentive to continual changes in life without being run by them. Indifference, on the other hand, connotes apathy, disinterest, even cold detachment to these changes. We feel joy when we receive undeserved acceptance and we feel sad, even angry, when there is rejection or outright hostility directed at us. An equanimous response is mindful of both of these experiences, neither craving nor aversive to them, while indifference takes the form of emotional bluntness to the point of uncaring.

I hope that with this distinction we can get a clearer sense of what I mean by equanimity and how it might support our desire to become a different sort of being so unlike before. Let me go a step further, though, in our discussion. According to the Buddhist tradition, the cultivation of equanimity or calm and steady disposition towards all experiences regardless of their emotional valence (e.g., pleasant, unpleasant, or neutral) is rooted in a particular insight regarding our relationship to four sets of contrasting conditions (dhammas).[7] These pairings, which we all have been subjected to at one point in our lives, include praise and blame, gain and loss, pleasure and pain, and fame and disrepute. The gay experience is often marked by the push-pull between these contrasting and dichotomous phenomena. There are times that we readily push away experiences of blame,

7. Liebenson, "Cultivating Equanimity."

loss, pain, and disrepute because of their adverse impact on our emotional lives and pull in with great might or intensity experiences of praise, gain, pleasure, and fame because of their intoxicating effects. The force of these experiences is so intense that we often feel powerless, and therefore succumb to them rather hastily. The cultivation of equanimity enables us to see deeply the impermanence and transitional nature of these conditions, and it makes explicit their embeddedness on the patterns of mimetic desires.

The concept of equanimity, though seldom spoken in Christian gatherings, is correlated with the gospel message of peace. Take, for example, the passage in Philippians 4:4–9, particularly its appeal for unity amidst strife and divisiveness in the church. By focusing their eyes on and rejoicing in the Lord "who is near" (vv. 4–6), their anxiety is supplanted by the "peace of God" (v. 7) that cannot be conjured up by human effort, but has its origin in God who calms and quiets the anxious mind.

Similarly, the perpetual conflict that is generated by the issue of homosexuality in the church has tainted and fractured relationships. It has made us all anxious in varying degrees and catapulted us to a war-like mentality with the other viewed as an enemy to defend against. Since God is in the midst of bringing forth a new creation and calling forth a new way of being and relating with one another, we can imbue and mirror this transcendent peace who is not in rivalry with anyone and therefore can relax and maintain a sense of equanimity while confronted by a contentious atmosphere. Instead of getting caught up in the emotional contagion that gets easily triggered by this issue we can turn our eyes on Jesus, our model of peace, and mimicking his own nonreactive and non-retaliatory stance. This is our way of embodying the faith so that through it we can make visible to the other the enlivening and non-judging presence of God in us. By "simply standing in a place of vulnerability we can invite someone to enter the sacred."[8] We remain engaged without getting entangled by the mimetic conflict as a way of making manifest the in-breaking of God in our midst.

Third, imitate God's self-giving love. As we discovered in earlier chapters, the shape and expression of our identity have been given to us through the unconscious process of mimesis. In other words, we are who we are because we are intricately connected to each other and therefore imitate each other's patterns of desire, mostly outside of our awareness. This started out very early in life when we were brought into existence by a relationship

8. Edman, *Queer Virtue*, 136.

that preceded us, our parents, and through them we get introduced to a particular way of being in the world via imitation.

As we grow and develop, we find ourselves inseparably linked to a much larger web of connections that shape who we are and define, even dictate, who we should become at times. As said previously, we are not autonomous, self-contained, and self-forming individuals, but are derivative and imitative creatures wholly dependent on others. Our identity is formed within the context of a "self-in-relation" caught up in the vortex of mimetic desire.

So, what does this have to do with this new and entirely different way of being with an entirely different source of identity that God is bringing forth in our midst? Everything! Since we are reflective and imitative creatures, we have the innate capacity to mirror the very character of God, who is love. The nature of this love is neither possessive nor rivalrous, but gratuitous and self-giving. And the more we "learn to desire through the eyes of another, so we are given the heart of another and what we learn is the extraordinarily benign, peaceful power of one holding everything in being, liking, and delighting in us, without distinction."[9] We can see ourselves through the eyes of God, who affirms our innate worth and takes pleasure in us just as we are, God's Beloved Queers. With God's regard and delight in us, we can embrace ourselves fully, wholeheartedly, and unconditionally. In the arms of a loving God, we lack nothing and therefore can relax, be at peace, and mirror back into the world the same "liking" of others, "without distinction."

In practical terms, this means, first of all, inclining the ears of our heart to hear the gentle whisper of God, whose image and likeness we bear, saying "this is my child who I really love so much." There is no ambivalence, conditionality, or double bind attached to this pronouncement. Just a pure and perhaps giddy declaration of how God truly feels towards us: "I really really like you."

Could you imagine the sort of persons we can become when we receive this new being from God whose unconditional, intimate, and loving regard for us is beyond doubt, never fails, and secure? Enamored and shaped by this love, we become loveable beings, meaning that as beloved we become lovers of others and, in the process, point them to the very source of that encompassing love. It is a kind of mimetic love that is so unlike what the world gives, which recreates and repeats patterns of desire that

9. Alison, *On Being Liked*, 16

excludes, is violent, and is life-negating. It is a kind of love that includes all and supports the shape or configuration of their flourishing.

This sounds a bit unrealistic, doesn't it? Can we actually embody this kind of love, self-giving and other-centered? By our own might and effort, of course, we cannot. But with God, nothing is impossible (Matt 19:26) because in Christ, who gives us strength, we can do all things (Phil 4:13). And there's more. Discovering ourselves on the inside of God's creative work, we realize that God is able to exceed our expectations and accomplish extraordinarily more than all we can imagine, think of, desire, or ask, for God Immanuel is at work within us (Eph 3:20).

Fourth, take an open stance towards God's unfolding and ongoing revelation. There is more to discover about this new being that you and I have been lured so delightfully to discover. We can now begin to imagine a future that is unsullied by pretensions, fear, cover-up, silence, and complicity in the scapegoat mechanism. In other words, the gates have been swung wide open, and we now have a chance to live freely, fully, and faithfully as heirs of a gratuitous God.

How does one cultivate this posture of openness, we might ask? Two things come to mind in response to this. The first one is open awareness or bare attention, which means becoming flexibly aware and attentive to whatever it is that enters into our field of perception.[10] Imagine standing on top of a mountain, overlooking a scenery that stretches beyond what our eyes could see. The mountain that grounds and holds us is the unshakeable regard of God towards us. It cannot be moved by the forces of scapegoating, but is nourished by the lush love that surrounds us all. Even when we falter, grow weary, and feel discouraged, remember that we are being held by someone who delights in us as we are. From this secure place, we are being given the eyes of faith to see and discover that God remains engaged, active, even relentless in bringing about a new creation that includes our own flourishing and those of others. And from this sense of security, we can begin to learn how to embrace discomfort, a "lack of ease with the available scripts for living and loving, along with the excitement in the face of the uncertainty of where the discomfort may take us."[11]

Often it is hard to recognize God's artistry in bringing about this new creation, especially when the name of God is used to blind us from seeing the unfolding of God's masterpiece. But God cannot be manipulated by

---

10. Nolasco, *Contemplative Counselor*, 78.

11. Ahmed, *Cultural Politics of Emotion*, 155.

religious piety or rhetoric or sacrifices (Hos 6:6), and instead acts in love by removing the scales off our eyes so that we can see clearly whose we are (as created in imago Dei) and who we are becoming (more like Christ). Such clarity enables us to see beyond the immediacy of our situation and into the wide-expanse of infinite human possibilities for growth and transformation (Isa 43) initiated and sustained by the very same God who created all there is out of nothing.

What anchors this open awareness is a particular kind of presence, an Open Presence that is marked by hospitality, curiosity, and loving-kindness. No longer driven by fear or shame or run by the need for approval and validation that closed us off and constricted our vision, we venture out into the world empowered to bear witness to the presence and power of God that is at work within us. The power of this transformative encounter cannot be contained or hidden. It will burst forth and bear the fruit of hospitality where there is aloofness, curiosity where there is fixity, and loving-kindness, especially in the midst of anger and hostility. As someone delightfully wanted, caringly held, and gratuitously adored by God, we embody this open presence, even in the midst of rejection and exclusion. We remain unfettered by the negativity around us, and we draw strength, resilience, and inspiration from the Forgiving Victim who, instead of retaliating, expressed love, understanding, and forgiveness towards the lynch mob. Through the presence and power of God that is at work within us, we can imitate this very example of Christ. Put another way, being God's Beloved necessitates that we love no matter what (John 12:34–35). Hence, the character of gay love is one that is steeped in the experience of the love of God.

Fifth, be vigilant or alert. In earlier chapters, we have established that the world we enter into is already caught up in mimetic contagion, which accounts for the conflicts and chaos, religious and otherwise, that we see around us. And when it comes to matters gay, there are already-established and deeply entrenched views from both sides of the divide even before we become aware of our sexuality. In other words, we have already been socialized, conditioned, and shaped by these narratives, and through the power of mimesis assimilate them unconsciously, especially at the beginning stages of our development. In our context, these narratives are so intricately fused with our sense of identity and belongingness that it is often difficult to critically question these received narratives. And since they are also drenched in religious language, it is often harder to challenge them.

But God's regard towards us transcends the limits of our imagination and the forces that try to "bind our conscience."[12] With the scales removed from our eyes, we can now see our divine image reflected back to us by God, who adores us as we are. With a transformed heart, we can now love as God loves, without conditions and manipulations. With a spirit set ablaze, we can now engage others not with timidity, hostility, or in rivalry, but with a quiet confidence in God's ongoing work in renewing all of creation.

As we participate in this new creation, we are admonished to remain vigilant and alert, as the devil, our adversary, is always on the lookout to devour its prey (1 Pet 5:8). Now, who is this enemy that we need to watch out for? Certainly not a personified figure with a horn and a fork, but a "principle of deceit" manifested in and sustained by actual structures of power and privilege that operate on the victimage mechanism.[13]

We know too well the devastating and damaging effects of this worldly operation, and how insidious it is when it comes to regulating human affairs. Alas, we are not forever chained to it. We have been released from this bondage by Christ, the Forgiving Victim. The trap that is mimetic violence is now supplanted by a life of mimetic grace.

In the process of shaking off the impact of this social mechanism, we will see traces of its impact on us. Residual feelings of rejection and shame or a lingering feeling of taking revenge in the name of social justice-making may from time to time bubble up from within us. Be vigilant and alert, as the enemy will take advantage of this vulnerability to seduce us back into a negative, destructive, cyclical mimesis. Instead, when these feelings are shored up, breathe slowly, gently, and deeply, then treat them as guests needing momentary shelter, bearing gifts for further exploration and healing.

Since we are still in the world, the principle of scapegoating, which energizes evil rulers and authorities and structures of powers, continues to ensnare people and communities into its deceptive and finger-pointing ways. Again, be vigilant and alert to its subtle or very unambiguous machinations, first by recognizing our own complicity in the scapegoat mechanism, and second by holding onto fiercely and making present, alive, and actual what the Forgiving Victim has accomplished for us on the cross, as declared in Ephesians 2.

---

12. Alison, *On Being Liked*, 100.

13. Rabe, *Desire Found Me*, loc. 2710.

For he himself is our peace, who has made the two groups one and has destroyed the barrier, the dividing wall of hostility, by setting aside in his flesh the law with its commands and regulations. His purpose was to create in himself one new humanity out of the two, thus making peace, and in one body to reconcile both of them to God through the cross, by which he put to death their hostility. He came and preached peace to you who were far away and peace to those who were near. For through him we both have access to the Father by one Spirit.

The peace of Christ that is within us cradles this call for vigilance. Without this peace, vigilance can turn into anxiety, making us more vulnerable to a defensive and reactive posture. Imbued with it, vigilance can make us see clearly what God is already doing in our midst, and through the Spirit of Christ we can partake of this reconciliatory work more actively and unanxiously. This includes the tearing down of walls that separate us and building of bridges that affirm our similarities (i.e., as image bearers of God) and celebrate our differences (i.e., the image takes myriad expressions).

Six, be sure to practice and offer the gift of empathy when engaging others in a conversation around matters gay. The issue of homosexuality remains a "hot button" issue that usually triggers a fight or flight response for many. When run by the feeling to defend against a perceived threat, the discourse becomes rivalrous, and a clear demarcation between us vs. them is thus drawn anew, creating a wedge with both sides firmly planted to defend their domain from their perceived enemy. With our propensity for mimesis, the emotional contagion spreads like wildfire, searing and blistering.

Showing empathy is a critical ingredient to remaining engaged without being drawn back into a mimetic contagion of attack and defend. But what is empathy and how might it further the conversation without scapegoating anyone? In simple terms, empathy is like walking in the shoes of another with genuine curiosity and keen interest. It reaches out in openness prompted only by a desire to understand, acknowledge, and respect the deep origins and complexity of someone's thoughts, feelings, and behaviors. It fosters vulnerability and honesty and a meeting of hearts and minds in unity without displacing or manipulating each other's differences and singularity. In this encounter, our shared humanity is affirmed and takes precedence and all else dissipates into the background.

More, empathy is wired in our brain. In a way, we are born this way, that is, we have the innate capacity to be interested in another, to intuit what they are feeling and thinking, and using that to promote pro-social behavior, reciprocity, cooperation, growth, and the flourishing of all. Parts of our brain, from mirror neurons to the left and right hemisphere down to our vagus nerves,[14] are all involved in orchestrating our social engagement system so that we can show empathy while remaining calm, attentive, attuned, and engaged when in dialogue with others about such complex and polarizing issues as homosexuality.

At this juncture, I would like to share with you a particular imaginal meditative practice that I hope would enhance your capacity for empathy. This is inspired by Donald Pfaff's Altruistic Brain Theory[15] (ABT), which I explored more fully in my other book.

Step One: Bring to mind a significant person in your life whom you want to share your life story with and who hasn't accepted you as you are. Imagine this person's face reflecting a life lived and a story that is layered just like yours. As you do this, notice how you breathe and then gradually settle into a gentle, slow, and deep diaphragmatic breathing.

Step Two: Imagine sitting across from this person in a relaxed muscle body and a calm, inviting, open stance. In your mind's eye imagine sharing a bit of your own story, your dreams, the struggles you have been facing, the suffering you are enduring, and your desire to be seen as a human being just like him or her. Notice how this feels in your heart. Do you feel light, at peace, and empowered? If so, lean into these feelings a bit more and draw courage and strength from them and your intention to share who you are with this person.

Now draw your attention to the other. Perhaps imagine how he or she might respond to your story. Whatever it is that you see, make sure that you remain calm and centered. As you look into this person's eye with a loving gaze, recite these words silently: "I want to get know you too, not as a rival, but as a fellow image bearer and recipients of God's liking, mercy, and compassion." Repeat these words a couple more times until they become a heartfelt prayer of intention.

Think of asking the following exploratory questions that I hope will spark a respectful dialogue or a genuine meeting of mind and heart:

14. Vittorio, "Action Recognition."
15. Pfaff, *Altruistic Brain*, 5.

1. What is it like to hear my story? How does it make you feel?

2. I know that you are struggling to accept who I am and that is alright. I respect that with no hard feelings. But I am interested to know how you have come to this place, to this conclusion about us, about our sexuality?

3. What are some of your fears, apprehensions, even concerns regarding who I am or who we are?

This is a difficult conversation to be had, and it is important to remain relaxed and engaging, open and curious throughout the process. The intention here is to listen to the other without judgment, to learn how to inhabit his or her subjective world in a respectful manner. This person, too, has a story, and whatever beliefs he or she may have about homosexuality are deeply personal and therefore worth listening to. Remember that this is not about persuasion, but it is an attempt to connect with the person and to extend an open hand and not a fist, as a non-retaliatory gesture for not accepting us.

Step Three: Bring to mind this person's face again and revel in the truth that he or she bears the image of God just like you. With a half-smile, look at this person lovingly, caringly, and compassionately, and imagine the love of God that is within you radiating outward, expanding, and embracing you both unreservedly and with delight.

Step Four: Lean into or linger a bit more in this flow of grace that makes possible an encounter with another that is anchored in empathic attunement and connection without expecting a particular outcome. Pay attention to how this feels in your heart and mind, and remember that empathy is about making room for another without the need to control or change the other.

Step Five: Do this exercise as frequent as possible and when you feel ready, I encourage you to invite this person to a conversation. Be not afraid! Take courage for God is with you! Fix your eyes not on the outcome but on the opportunity to reflect back what it means to love in the midst of rejection, to stay true to who we are even though that truth is challenged and dismissed.

Finally, dare greatly and boldly! This is the culmination of a series of soul habits I have outlined above. With our heart, mind, and body in sync and energized, our identity as God's beloved firmly established, and patterns of desire transformed into imitating the very desires of God, life as we know it may never be the same, perhaps not in outward appearances, but in the quality of how this life might be lived out.

So, I dare each one of us to imagine our lives with only one single purpose, that is, to gaze on the beauty of the Lord (Ps 27:4; Luke 10:42), who adores you, and with these eyes see the beauty in others as well. There is no rivalry, sense of lack, need for a scapegoat, or anxious and fearful feeling when we are able to see beyond the masks and hurts and recognize the divine image in each of us. Internalized beauty overflows and seamlessly catches and affirms the beauty in others.

I dare each of us to imagine what peacemaking may look like in our own unique context. Following the way of Jesus means practicing nonviolence and reconciliation right where we are, wherever that may be. Compassionate and non-retaliatory engagement blossoms not in avoidance of suffering, but in working through it with others. Like water lilies growing in the mud, peacemaking entails being embedded in places where there are conflicts and deep hurts, and otherization is at play. This means actively resisting attempts of scapegoating, empowering and advocating for those whose voice has been silenced or dismissed, and extending grace and lovingkindness to ourselves and others, especially when we all fail to incarnate and mirror the love of God to each other.

I dare each of us to imagine curating the shape of our own flourishing. We all are very unique in our way. God delights in this one and only version of ourselves. So, as we embark on this, bear in mind that our God is the God of infinite possibilities and our life's trajectory is within the purview of the One who makes impossible possible. Hence, let us allow ourselves to flourish in the most authentic expression of the image of God in each of us, to have that kind of vision that befits who we are and what we are meant to be. I believe that God's love for the beloved anticipates a future that is full of possibilities to become the sort of person we are created to be. Discovering what that looks like in the concreteness of our lives now and into the future is the adventure in which we are called to participate. So, dare to dream and dare big!

You may have already noticed this, but if you string together the first letter of these soul habits, you will find the word "beloved." In this context, our belovedness not only defines who we are in the eyes of God. It also describes what we do in light of this bestowed identity. So, let us be lovers of God, ourselves, and others, because that truly is a mark of God's Beloved Queers.

I will leave you with several guided spiritual habits that I hope will enrich and support your journey towards sustained affirmation and celebration of your queer identity, whose very existence is a queer reflection of God.

Spiritual Habit #1: God's Compassion

Tending the Body

Sit in a comfortable position in a quiet space. Place your hands on your lap with your palms facing up. Close your eyes and notice the rhythm of your breathing.

Is it shallow and short? Deep and gentle? Whatever it is, simply become aware of the sensation of your breathing.

Slowly and gently, take a few deep breaths in through your nose and breathe out through pursed lips as if you were whistling. Settle here for a moment and let your body breathe you (yes, let your body do what it needs to do—*breathe*).

Notice the sounds you hear about you. Listen first for the fainter, more distant sounds, then those that are nearby. Simply become aware of them. Whenever you find yourself getting lost in your head or distracted, there is no problem, no judgment, no shame. Just gently draw your attention back to the sensation of your breathing.

Now draw your attention to the middle portion of your chest—to your heart. While breathing, mindfully imagine inclining your ears to your heart and listen to its heartbeat.

Notice the deepening sound of silence in this place of prayer.

Listen to the word of the Lord: "Be still and know that I am God." (Ps 46:10a)

Tending the Mind

In the state of calm, read the following verses taken from Mark 6:30–34, slowly and gently. Try to savor each word or phrase, let it rest in your heart. As the passage settles within, be mindful of the still, small voice of God inviting you to enter deeply into God's presence.

The apostles gathered around Jesus and reported to him all they had done and taught. Then, because so many people were coming and going that they did not even have a chance to eat, he said to them, "Come with me by yourselves to a quiet place and get some rest. So, they went away by themselves in a boat to a solitary place. But many who saw them leaving recognized them and ran on foot from all the towns and got there ahead of them. When Jesus landed and saw a large crowd, he had compassion on them, because they were like without a shepherd. So, he began teaching them many things.

Follow these instructions.

- Read the above text two more times, slowly and gently.

- Take a word or phrase or an image that caught your attention. Ponder it, memorize it, and slowly repeat it to yourself, perhaps in sync with your breathing. Allow it to speak to your inner world, be open to its direction, receive it with hospitality, and converse with it.

- Speak to God, either in words or images, whatever is emerging for you at this time. Then, listen deeply to what God may be inviting you to meditate further. Write all the salient ideas that are surfacing for you in your personal journal.

- Reflect on this question: In what way does this meditative exercise intersect with my evolving story as a queer person who bears the image and likeness of God?

- Stay close to your experience, noting thoughts, feelings, and sensations as you write your response to the question above. As best as you can, don't make any judgments on what you are writing about. Try not to analyze or interpret them, as well. Just simply be a witness to your own experience.

- When finished, take a few deep mindful breaths.

Tending the Spirit

End this first spiritual habit with a guided meditation.

- Sit in a comfortable chair in a quiet space, eyes either slightly open or gently closed. Place your hands on your lap with your palms facing up. Take a few deep breaths.

- Become mindful or aware of the air that is coming into and going out of your body, of your chest expanding during the in-breath and collapsing on out-breath. Linger here for a moment.

- Whenever you find yourself getting lost in your head or getting overwhelmed, there is no problem, no judgment, no shame. Gently draw your attention back to the sensation of breathing.

- Now picture yourself in the crowd towards whom Jesus saw and felt compassion. Notice his face, his eyes and imagine him walking towards you. You feel his tenderness, warmth, and open stance. You experience his nearness and the assurance that he is there with you so eager to touch and heal your aching heart, stifled spirit, distressed body, and broken relationships.

- While continuing to breathe mindfully, you hear the words of Christ: "Come to me all of you who are weary and I will give you rest" (Matt 11:28). Linger here for a moment and internalize or take in the words spoken to you so lovingly and caringly.

- As you consent to this invitation, you become aware of aspects of your life that needs the compassionate touch of God. Name them one by one and offer them up to God in humility, reverence, and submission.

- Let the warmth of God's compassion lift your burdens up to make you feel light, accompanied, strengthened, and assured. With a half-smile, linger here for a moment and try to immerse yourself fully into this experience of God's "with-ing" amidst your suffering and in the concreteness of your life.

- In the last few minutes, take a few deep breaths and turn your attention again to the sensation of your breathing. When ready, you can open your eyes if they have been closed and direct a loving gaze outward and into the rest of your day.[16]

End this time of fellowship with God with this prayer.

> Lord, I freely yield all my liberty to you.
> Take my memory, my intellect, and my entire will.
> You have given me everything I am or have;
> I give it all back to you to stand under your will alone.

16. Nolasco, *Compassionate Presence*, 88.

Your love and your grace are enough for me;
I shall ask for nothing more.[17]

—Saint Ignatius of Loyola (1491–1556)

Spiritual Habit #2: Invitation to Fellowship

Tending the Body

Sit in a comfortable position in a quiet space. Place your hands on your lap with your palms facing up. Close your eyes and notice the rhythm of your breathing.

Is it shallow and short? Deep and gentle? Whatever it is, simply become aware of the sensation of your breathing.

Slowly and gently, take a few deep breaths in through your nose and breathe out through pursed lips as if you were whistling. Settle here for a moment and let your body breathe you (yes, let your body do what it needs to do—*breathe*).

As you breathe in, say the first part of the Jesus Prayer: "Lord, Jesus Christ" (or any phrase that is most meaningful to you). As you do this, imagine that you are breathing into yourself the love, grace, and presence of the Lord Jesus. As you breathe out, say the second part of the prayer: "Have mercy on me" (or any phrase that is most meaningful to you). Imagine you are breathing out of yourself all your cares and worries, anything that gets in the way of your openness to God's mercy and grace.

Continue to breathe in the words "Lord Jesus Christ," and breathe out the words "Have mercy on me" for another minute or so. When you are ready to come out of the silence, open your eyes and direct your attention outward.

Tending the Mind

One of the ways of cultivating worshipful attention to God is praying with icons. Using icons to deepen one's prayer life is quite common among Christians, particularly those of the Eastern Orthodox tradition. The two-dimensional sacred art inspires us to be still, to behold, to gaze upon, to

17. Storey, *Book of Prayer*, 63

pray, to be fully present with and attentive to what is represented for us. With our eyes fixed on the icon, in quiet and prayerful anticipation, we see beyond the image and penetrate the depths of what it symbolizes.

This spiritual habit uses the ancient Byzantine icon called "The Holy Trinity" created by the monk Andrei Rublev in 1425. The icon is a representation of an event recorded in Genesis 18 known as the "hospitality of Abraham." It omits the characters of Abraham, Sarah, and the servants in order to focus our attention solely on the images of three angels seated at the table, which takes us into the mysterious relationship within the Trinity between the Father, the Son, and the Holy Spirit.

"The Trinity" by Andrei Rublev
The Tretyakov Gallery, Moscow, Russia

In the next seven minutes or so, you will spend some time praying with the icon. In this exercise, praying means waiting and listening in silence.

- To begin, make sure that the icon is downloaded or displayed in your screen in color so you can see all of its details. Light a candle, if you would like.

- Explore the icon with your eyes and with your feelings. Pause and consider the feelings it brings up in you. Simply sit with the icon, mindfully and prayerfully looking at it, really seeing it.

- Now draw your attention to the Christ figure seated at the center of the icon. Notice the crimson and blue color of the garment and other details that may catch your attention.

- When ready, turn your attention to the figure on the right, the God-the-Father figure, notice the creation colors of blue and green, and simply sit with it and let it speak to you.

- From there, turn your gaze to the figure on the left, the Holy-Spirit figure. Notice the transparent color, and then ask the Spirit to guide you during this prayerful meditation

- Notice how the Son sits at the right hand of the Father, who nods towards him. The Son, in turn inclines his head to the Holy Spirit. Attend to this circular visual moment and receive what this might symbolize for you.

- Lastly, draw your attention to what seems to be a "eucharistic table" and the hand of the Christ-figure making a welcoming gesture. As you spend some time gazing upon this part of the icon, reflect on the following:

Many times, the queer community has been silenced, restricted, and expelled from participating fully in the religious life of our faith community. And often, this exclusion has been accorded with the status of divine truth. But God has got nothing to do with this sacred violence, and is over against nothing and no one at all. God is for us and loves us as we are, wherever we are in this faith journey.

In light of this, draw your attention back to the centerpiece of the icon, with the Christ figure signaling a welcoming gesture to join the Trinity in their intimate fellowship. Sit with this image for a while and then, when ready, reflect on the following:

- What feelings and thoughts are bubbling up inside of me as I sit with God's invitation for intimate fellowship? Is there excitement or eagerness? Reservation or tentativeness?

- Whatever it is, write a letter to God expressing what your feelings and thoughts are about this experience while breathing mindfully, deeply, and prayerfully.

Tending the Spirit

End this time of fellowship with God by reciting the Jesus Prayer in concert with your breathing. Breathe in the words "Lord Jesus Christ." Breathe out the words "Have mercy on me."

Spiritual Habit #3: Self-Compassion

Tending the Body

Sit in a comfortable position in a quiet space. Place your hands on your lap with your palms facing up. Close your eyes and notice the rhythm of your breathing.

Is it shallow and short? Deep and gentle? Whatever it is, simply become aware of the sensation of your breathing.

Slowly and gently, take a few deep breaths in through your nose and breathe out through pursed lips as if you were whistling. Settle here for a moment and let your body breathe you (yes, let your body do what it needs to do—*breathe*).

Now bring to mind a layout of your day—tasks that need to be carried out, people to connect with, and other activities that need your careful attention, significant or trivial, one by one. Simply become aware of them, and as best as you can, refrain from strategizing or planning how you will approach these activities.

Whenever you find yourself getting lost in your head or distracted, there is no problem, no judgment, no shame. Just gently draw your attention back to the sensation of your breathing.

As you begin to settle in your breathing once more, become aware of feelings, bodily sensations, and thoughts that begin to emerge. Treat them like clouds passing by your consciousness and simply acknowledge them. Label these feelings, name these thoughts, and locate where these bodily sensations are coming from.

Then, in a posture of prayer, incline the ears of your heart and listen to these words: "In all your ways acknowledge the Lord and the Lord will make your paths straight" (Prov 3:6). With a half-smile, linger here for a moment, and in faith anticipate the unfolding of God's presence in your midst.

In the last minute or so, take a few deep breaths and turn your attention again to the sensation pf your breathing. When ready, you can open your eyes if they have been closed and draw your attention outward with heartfelt intention and attention.[18]

Tending the Mind

In this state of calm, read the following directions and respond accordingly. In your journal, draft a letter to your body in which you express your gratitude for the ways it has supported or protected you or helped you heal, learning things, or enjoy yourself. Also, write down your disappointments about the ways you feel it has let you down, failed you, or held you back. Think about your earliest memories and describe the appreciations and disappointments you felt at that time, and then progress chronologically though your history up to the present moment in your adult life.[19]

When ready, take a few deep breaths and then draw your attention to the following verse from John 1:1–5 and 14. Read it slowly and gently while breathing mindfully.

> In the beginning was the Word, and the Word was with God, and the word was God. He was with God in the beginning. Through him all things were made; without him nothing was made that has been made. In him was life, and that life was the light of all mankind. The light shines, and darkness has not overcome it.

> The Word became flesh and made his dwelling among us.

Put the letter you just wrote next to the verses you just read, reread both them, if need be, and then reflect on the following question.

- Does the incarnation of Christ, of God entering into materiality by taking on human flesh, make a difference in how we experience and relate to our queer bodies? If so, in what way?

18. Nolasco, *Compassionate Presence*, 81.
19. Ogden and Fisher, *Sensorimotor Psychotherapy*, 86.

- Write down any reflections you have about the question. As best as you can, don't make any judgments on what you are writing about. Try not to analyze or interpret them, as well. Just simply be a witness to your own experience.

- When finished, take a few deep mindful breathes.

Tending the Spirit

End this spiritual habit with a guided meditation.

- Sit in a comfortable chair in a quiet space, eyes either slightly open or gently closed. Place your hands on your lap with your palms facing up. Take a few deep breaths.

- Become aware of the air that is coming into and going out of your body, of your chest expanding during the in-breath and collapsing on out-breath. Linger here for a moment.

- Whenever you find yourself getting lost in your head or getting overwhelmed, there is no problem, no judgment, no shame. Gently draw your attention back to the sensation of breathing.

- Now picture yourself in the crowd that Jesus saw and felt compassion towards. Notice his face, his eyes, and imagine him walking towards you. You feel his tenderness, warmth, and open stance. You experience his nearness, and the assurance that he is there with you.

- While continuing to breathe mindfully, imagine offering jarred pieces of your broken self to Christ—your insecurity about your body, fear of failure and rejection, your self-doubt and feeling of being unwanted, unloved, and not cared for.

- Notice how you feel when you surrender these broken pieces to God. Do you feel lighter, made whole, and loved unconditionally?

- As you gaze upon his face you hear the words: "I will give thanks to you, for I am delicately and wonderfully made. Wonderful are your works, and my souls knows it very well" (Ps 139:14).

- Now place your right hand on your heart while letting these words echo deep within your heart. Lean into these words and notice how you feel. Do you feel any sensation? Do you feel deeply loved, cared for, accepted, and intimately close to the source of this love?

- If not, that is fine. No judgment, no problem, no shame. Just focus on the sensation of your breathing or the loving face of Christ or the words spoken earlier, and breathe mindfully.

- With a half-smile, silently recite to yourself the following phrase:

  > May I feel the love of Christ for me.
  > May this love heal those broken pieces of myself and make me whole.
  > May I know in my heart and mind that I am God's Beloved.
  > That I am deeply loved just as I am.

- Breathe and silently repeat these words two more times.

- Again, notice how this feels in your heart. Did you notice any change in how you feel and think about yourself? Are you beginning to see yourself the way God sees you? If so, bathe yourself in this intimate knowing that God loves you as you are.

- In the last few minutes, take a few deep breaths and turn your attention again to the sensation of your breathing. When ready, you can open your eyes if they have been closed and direct a loving gaze outward and into the rest of your day.[20]

Spiritual Habit #4: Self-Compassion Towards an Anxious Part

Tending the Body

Sit in a comfortable position in a quiet space. Place your hands on your lap with your palms facing up. Close your eyes and notice the rhythm of your breathing.

Is it shallow and short? Deep and gentle? Whatever it is, simply become aware of the sensation of your breathing.

Slowly and gently, take a few deep breaths in through your nose and breathe out through pursed lips as if you were whistling. Settle here for a moment and let your body breathe you (yes, let your body do what it needs to do—*breathe*).

Notice the sounds you hear about you. Listen first for the fainter, more distant sounds, then those that are nearby. Simply become aware of them. Whenever you find yourself getting lost in your head or distracted, there is

20. Nolasco, *Compassionate Presence*, 92–93.

no problem, no judgment, no shame. Just gently draw your attention back to the sensation of your breathing.

Now draw your attention to the middle portion of your chest—to your heart. While breathing, mindfully imagine inclining your ears to your heart and listen to its heartbeat. Notice the deepening sound of silence in this place of prayer. Listen to the word of the Lord: "Be still and know that I am God" (Ps 46:10a).

Tending the Mind

In the state of calm and while breathing mindfully, read the following:

Repeated exposure to the normative discourse on homosexuality (or other life-altering events for that matter) evokes feelings of anxiety that are often accompanied by bodily sensations (muscle tension, headache, dizziness, edginess, shortness of breath) and negative thoughts. Perhaps many of us have been able to find freedom from internalizing these messages as our own and found ways to self-soothe or regulate these anxious feelings. However, others may still be struggling with a low grade but lingering feelings of anxiousness, especially when exposed to a trigger.

Cultivating an attitude of mindfulness—or awareness and attention to this lingering anxious feeling with curiosity and non-judgment—will help foster a different way of responding to feelings of anxiety. Neither denying or being managed by this feeling, we engage this feeling with hospitality, like a "guest bearing gift" for further exploration and healing.

As you get acquainted with this feeling, please bring to mind and practice the Self-Compassion Spiritual Habit #3 you've learned previously, as it is only through a positive emotional stance that we can begin to develop a different stance towards these negative or unpleasant feelings.

Anxious Feelings	Compassion	Anxious Thoughts
Getting Clarity: Identify the most accurate "anxious feeling label" that best captures your internal experience: Insecure, Helpless, Worried, Apprehensive, Anxious, Afraid, Ashamed, Humiliated, Guilty, Depressed, Vulnerable, Suspicious	Practice Self-Compassion	Getting Clarity: Identify an ANT, or automatic negative thought, that comes with feelings of anxiety. An ANT is a stream of negative and critical judgments about ourselves that either induces or exacerbates feelings of anxiety. ANT: *"I am no good"*

Bring to mind a recent situation when you felt anxious. Then, using the table above, identify the following:

- Feeling (at rock bottom). Choose from the list above.

- Automatic Negative Thought

While practicing "self-compassion" towards this anxious part, reflect on the question

- What is this feeling of anxiety (or insecurity, worry, shame, sadness) inviting me to reflect further? Write them down on your journal.

- What biblical images, symbols, or verses come to mind that might help clarify, provide encouragement and direction, even transform this feeling? Write them down.

- Speak to God, either in words or images—whatever is emerging for you at this time.

- Then, listen deeply to what God may be inviting you to meditate on further or act upon.

Tending the Spirit

End this spiritual habit with a guided meditation.

- Sit in a comfortable chair in a quiet space, eyes either slightly open or gently closed. Place your hands on your lap with your palms facing up. Take a few deep breaths.

- Become mindful or aware of the air that is coming into and going out of your body, of your chest expanding during the in-breath and collapsing on out-breath. Linger here for a moment.

- Whenever you find yourself getting lost in your head or getting over-whelmed, there is no problem, no judgment, no shame. Gently draw your attention back to the sensation of breathing.

- Get in touch with your compassionate self—the part of you that is secure and rooted in God's love for you, that reminds you of your belovedness despite of your flaws and shortcomings. Identify with and lean into the innate qualities of your compassionate self—empathic, accepting, awake, benevolent (especially in the face of suffering), and mindful at all times. Linger here for a moment until you experience the warm embrace of your compassionate self.

- Now bring to mind a time when you were feeling anxious, tense, nervous, scared, or uneasy. Or if you are sensing those feelings right now, at this moment, that is all right, too. Just remember that you are looking at that anxious part of you through the eyes of your compassionate self.

- Give yourself permission to feel connected with that feeling of anxiety while you remain grounded in the qualities of your compassionate self. Try to locate that feeling in your body as you continue to breathe mindfully. Do you feel it in your chest, or shoulders, or stomach?

- Place your hand gently on that part of your body where you feel anxious, as if cradling or soothing an agitated child. Then breathe through your anxiety gently, slowly, and with empathy.

- While remaining anchored in your compassionate self, begin to think of the anxiety as a guest bearing a gift or a message. What does this feeling want you to know? What is this feeling needing from you—Validation? Understanding? Acknowledgement? Resolution?

Whatever it is, let the compassionate self be your guide as you deepen your awareness and understanding of this feeling.

- Now see yourself in your mind's eye, and then, with a half-smile, offer these words to that part of you that feels anxious

   [Say your name], may you be free of anxiety.
   May you be free of worries and fears.
   May you experience the peace of Christ that makes you well and whole.

- Say these words two more times, gently, slowly, expectantly, again letting compassion flow from your compassionate self to your anxious self. Linger here for moment while you breathe mindfully.

- Notice how this feels in your heart. Do you feel less anxious, light, at peace? If so, bathe yourself in this peaceful state. If not, that's all right; no judgment, no shame, and no problem. Just remain connected to your intention to be kind and compassionate to that part of you.

- In the last few minutes, take a few deep breaths and turn your attention again to the sensation of your breathing. When ready, you can open your eyes if they have been closed and direct a loving gaze outward and let the peace radiate from the inside out.[21]

Spiritual Habit #5: Compassion towards a Neighbor

Tending the Body

Sit in a comfortable position in a quiet space. Place your hands on your lap with your palms facing up. Close your eyes and notice the rhythm of your breathing.

Is it shallow and short? Deep and gentle? Whatever it is, just simply become aware of the sensation of your breathing.

Slowly and gently, take a few deep breaths in through your nose and breathe out through pursed lips as if you were whistling. Settle here for a moment and let your body breathe you (yes, let your body do what it needs to do—*breathe*).

21. Nolasco, *Compassionate Presence*, 94.

As you breathe in, say the first part of the Jesus Prayer: "Lord, Jesus Christ" (or some variation that is most meaningful). As you do this, imagine that you are breathing into yourself the love, grace, and presence of the Lord Jesus. As you breathe out, say the second part of the prayer: "Have mercy on me" (or some variation). Imagine you are breathing out of yourself all your cares and worries, anything that gets in the way of your openness to God's mercy and grace.

Breathe in the words "Lord, Jesus Christ"; breathe out the words "Have mercy on me."

When you are ready to come out of the silence, open your eyes and direct your attention outward.

Tending the Mind

This spiritual practice today involves a rereading of the parable of the Good Samaritan in Luke 10:25–37. This will be followed by reflecting on Vincent van Gogh's painting of the same name.

- Read Luke 10:25–37 prayerfully, while breathing mindfully (deeply, slowly, gently).

- When ready, spend some time looking at van Gogh's painting.

- Notice the first two characters on the left side of the painting. One is further up by the tree, and the other is down below next to an empty chest reading a book. Take note of the dull and muted colors that blend seamlessly into the background.

"The Good Samaritan," Vincent van Gogh
Kroller-Muller Museum, The Netherlands

- Then draw your attention to the center piece of the painting. Here, you will see the Samaritan and the wounded man front and center. Their bodies intertwined or joined together. The Samaritan's back is slightly arched, and with force and intensity he lifts the man onto his donkey. Take note of the vibrant red gear, bright golden cloak, and brilliant blue tunic, which the Samaritan shared with the man to cover his nakedness.

- Sit with the passage and the painting a bit more, and let them open up and inhabit your imagination.

- Attend and make note of whatever thoughts and feelings arise within you while you do this. When ready reflect on the following:

- Who among the characters in the story do we identify with?

- Who were the Good Samaritans in our lives who showed unconditional love, mercy, and compassion during those difficult times when we experienced rejection, exclusion, and banishment because of our sexuality? What is it like to be cared for lovingly by someone whose generosity relieved our own suffering?

- How might we cultivate an attitude of neighborly love towards others and become attentive to their inner turmoil?

Tending the Spirit

End this time with reciting the Jesus Prayer in concert with your breathing. Breathe in the words "Lord Jesus Christ" and breathe out the words "Have mercy on me."

- Sit in a comfortable chair in a quiet space, eyes either slightly open or gently closed. Place your hands on your lap with your palms facing up. Take a few deep breaths.

- Become mindful or aware of the air that is coming into and going out of your body, of your chest rising during the in-breath and collapsing on out-breath. Linger here for a moment.

- Whenever you find yourself getting lost in your head or distracted, no problem, no judgment, and no shame. Gently draw your attention back to the sensation of breathing.

- Bring to mind a time or a situation when you felt judged, looked down upon, criticized, spoken negatively about, or harmed because you are gay. Let whatever feelings surface and be present to them. As best as you can, try not to judge yourself or be swayed or managed by their strength. Breathe through these feelings and acknowledge them for what they are—your emotional responses to the pain and suffering to which you have been subjected. You may feel anger towards them, and for good reason; that is perfectly appropriate and understandable. Be mindful of these feelings and breathe through them as you become conscious of them.

- Now get in touch with your compassionate self—the part of you that is secure and rooted in God's love for you, that reminds you of your belovedness despite of how other people may treat or relate to you. Identify with and lean into the innate qualities of your compassionate self—empathic, accepting, awake, benevolent especially in the face of suffering, and mindful at all times. Linger here for a moment until you experience the warm embrace of your compassionate self.

- Imagine the face of the person who did you wrong. Look deeply into his/her eyes and become aware of this person's story and history. Reflect on how much his/her social context, cultural upbringing, religious affiliation, and his/her own vulnerabilities, insecurities, fears, ignorance, and own suffering has shaped and contributed to his/her prejudicial and damaging behaviors. As you reflect on these things, pay attention to whatever feelings may surface within you and attend to them with curiosity and hospitality. Let your compassionate self be the vessel of these feelings, and let this part of you offer the strength and inspiration that you need to offer these words to this person.

> [Say the person's name], may you be free from the destructive effects of hatred and hostility.
> May you see and appreciate the sacred worth and image of God in each person.
> May you radiate love, acceptance, and kindness to all.

- Repeat this prayer two more times and let these words take root in your heart and mind. As you end this time of meditation, think of a very tangible way of extending grace, forgiveness, and compassion towards this person.
- In the last few minutes, take a few deep breaths and turn your attention again to the sensation of your breathing. When ready, you can open your eyes if they have been closed and direct a loving compassionate gaze outward and into the rest of your day.

In closing, I would like to leave you again with this affirmation.

> Yes, you are loved as you are!
> And your love is as pure and genuine and true as the love of another!
> So, let us celebrate this love,
> Love that mirrors the consummate love of Christ,
> A victimless, gratuitous, and creative love
> That declares with such delightful cheer that
> You are, without a doubt,
> God's Beloved Queer!

> *Soli Deo Gloria.*

Bibliography

Adam, Rebecca. "Loving Mimesis and Girard's 'Scapegoat of the Text': A Creative Reassessment of Mimetic Desire." In *Violence Renounced: René Girard, Biblical Studies, and Peacemaking*, edited by Willard M. Swartley, 277–307. Studies in Peace and Scripture 4. Telford: Pandora, 2000.

Ahmed, Sarah. *The Cultural Politics of Emotion*. New York: Routledge, 2004.

Alison, James. *Broken Hearts and New Creations*. London: Continuum, 2010.

———. *Faith Beyond Resentment: Fragments Catholic and Gay*. New York: The Crossroad, 2015.

———. *Jesus the Forgiving Victim: Listening for the Unheard Voice*. Glenview: Doers, 2013.

———. *The Joy of Being Wrong: Original Sin through Easter Eyes*. New York: Crossroad, 1998.

———. *Knowing Jesus*. London: SPCK Classics, 2012.

———. *On Being Liked*. New York: The Crossroad, 2016.

———. *Undergoing God: Dispatches from the Scene of a Break-in*. London: Continuum, 2006.

Althaus-Reid, Marcella. *Indecent Theology: Theological Perversions in Sex, Gender, and Politics*. New York: Routledge, 2000.

Audlin, James David. *The Gospel of John: The Original Version Restored and Translated with Commentaries*. Vol. 2, *Commentaries on the Text*. Paso Ancho: Panama, 2014.

Bailie, Gil. *Violence Unveiled: Humanity at the Crossroads*. New York: Crossroad, 1995.

Bakshi, Sandeep, et al. *Decolonizing Sexualities: Transnational Perspective Critical Interventions*. Oxford: Counter, 2016.

Baldock, Kathy. *Walking the Bridgeless Canyon: Repairing the Breach Between the Church and the LGBT Community*. Reno: Canyon Walker, 2014.

Baptism, Eucharist and Ministry: Faith and Order Paper No. 111. Geneva: WCC, 1982. https://www.anglicancommunion.org/media/102580/lima_document.pdf.

Becker, Ernest. *The Structure of Evil: An Essay on the Unification of the Science of Man*. New York: Braziller, 1968.

Bowlby, John. *Attachment*. Vol 1, *Attachment and Loss*. New York: Basic Books, 1982.

Boswell, John. *Christianity, Social Tolerance, and Homosexuality: Gay People in Western Europe from the Beginning of the Christian Era to the Fourteenth Century*. Chicago: University Chicago Press.

Butler, Judith. *Gender Trouble: Feminism and the Subversion of Identity*. Abingdon: Routledge, 2006.

———. *Undoing Gender*. New York: Routledge, 2004.

Cheng, Patrick. *Radical Love: An Introduction to Queer Theology*. New York: Seabury, 2011.

Cikara, Mina, et al. "Us and Them: Intergroup Failures of Empathy." *Current Directions in Psychological Science* 20 (2011) 149–53.

Cobb, Michael. *God Hates Fags: The Rhetorics of Religious Violence*. New York: New York University Press, 2006.

Collins, Robin. "Girard and Atonement: An Incarnational Theory of Mimetic Participation." and *Violence Renounced: René Girard, Biblical Studies, and Peacemaking*, edited by Willard M. Swartley, 132–50. Studies in Peace and Scripture 4. Telford: Pandora, 2000.

Comstock, Gary David. *Gay Theology Without Apology*. Cleveland: Pilgrim, 1993.

Comstock, Gary David, and Susan E. Henking, eds. *Queerying Religion: A Critical Anthology*. New York, Continuum, 1997.

Csikszentmihalyi, Mihaly. *Flow: The Psychology of Optimal Experience*. New York: Harper Perennial, 2008.

Delamater John F., et al. "Essentialism vs. Social Constructionism in the Study of Human Sexuality." *Journal of Sex Research* 35 (1998) 10–13.

Desbordes, Gaëlle, et al. "Moving beyond Mindfulness: Defining Equanimity as an Outcome Measure in Meditation and Contemplative Research." *Mindfulness* 6 (2015) 356–72.

Diamond, Irene, and Lee Quinby, eds. *Feminism and Foucault: Reflections on Resistance*. Lebanon: Northeastern University Press, 1988.

Dormor, Duncan, and Jeremy Morris. *An Acceptable Sacrifice? Homosexuality and the Church*. London: SPCK, 2007.

Edman, Elizabeth M. *Queer Virtue: What LGBTQ People Know about Life and Love and How It Can Revitalize Christianity*. Boston: Beacon, 2016.

Esptein, Seymour. *Cognitive-Experiential Theory: An Integrative Theory of Personality*. Oxford: Oxford University Press, 2014.

Finley, James. *The Awakening Call: Fostering Intimacy with God*. Notre Dame: Ave Maria, 1984.

Flemming, Dean. *Philippians: A Commentary in the Wesleyan Tradition*. Kansas City: Beacon Hill, 2009.

Foucault, Michel. *The History of Sexuality, Vol. 1: An Introduction*. New York: Vintage, 1990.

Garrels, Scott. "Imitation, Mirror Neurons, and Mimetic Desire: Convergence between the Mimetic Theory of René Girard and Empirical Research on Imitation." *Contagion: Journal of Violence, Mimesis, and Culture* 12/13 (2006) 49–86.

Garrels, Scott, ed. *Mimesis and Science: Empirical Research on Imitation and the Mimetic Theory of Culture and Religion*. East Lansing: Michigan University Press, 2011.

Girard, René. "Generative Scapegoating." In *Violent Origins: Walter Burket, René Girard, and Jonathan Smith on Ritual Killing and Cultural Foundations*, edited by Robert G. Hammerton-Kelly, 73–148. Palo Alto: Stanford University Press, 1988.

———. *The Girard Reader*. Edited by James Williams. New York: Crossroad, 1976.

———. *Violence and the Sacred*. New York. Norton, 1979.

———. *Things Hidden Since the Foundation of the World*. Palo Alto: Stanford University Press, 1987.

Grawe, Klaus. *Neuropsychotherapy: How the Neurosciences Inform Effective Psychotherapy*. New York: Taylor & Francis, 2017.

Grimsurd, Ted. "Scapegoating No More: Christian Pacifism and New Testament View of Jesus Death." In *Violence Renounced: René Girard, Biblical Studies, and Peacemaking*, edited by Willard M. Swartley, 49–69. Studies in Peace and Scripture 4. Telford: Pandora, 2000.

Halperin, David M. "The Normalization of Queer Theory." *Journal of Homosexuality* 45 (2003) 339–43.

———. *One Hundred Years of Homosexuality*. New York: Routledge, 1990.

Hammerton-Kelly, Robert. *Sacred Violence*. Minnesota: Fortress, 1992.

Happold, F. C. *Mysticism: A Study and an Anthology*. London: Penguin, 1973.

Hart, David Bently. *The New Testament: A Translation*. New Haven: Yale University Press, 2017.

Job, Rueben, and Neil M. Alexander, eds. *Finding Our Way: Love and Law in the United Methodist Church*. Nashville: Abingdon, 2014.

John of the Cross, Saint. *The Ascent of Mount Carmel and the Dark Night*. Translated by John Venrad. Darlington: Darlington Carmel, 1981.

Juergensmeyer, Mark. *Terror in the Mind of God: The Global Rise of Religious Violence*. Los Angeles: University of California Press, 2001.

Kazen, Thomas. *Emotions in Biblical Law: A Cognitive Science Approach*. Sheffield: Sheffield Phoenix, 2011.

Kinsman, Gary. *The Regulation of Desire: Homo and Hetero Sexualities*. 2nd ed. New York: Black Rose, 1992.

Kringelbach, Morten, et al. "The Neuroscience of Happiness and Pleasure." *Social Research* 77 (2010) 659–78.

Kuefler, Mathew. *The Boswell Thesis: Essays on Christianity, Social Tolerance, and Homosexuality*. Chicago: University Chicago Press, 2006.

Liebenson, Narayan. "Cultivating Equanimity." *Insight* (Spring 1999) 42–43. https://www.buddhistinquiry.org/article/cultivating-equanimity-2/.

Loughlin, Gerard, ed. *Queer Theology: Rethinking the Western Body*. Hoboken: Wiley-Blackwell, 2007.

McGilchrist, Ian. *The Master and the His Emmisary: The Divided Brain and the Making of the Western World*. New Haven: Yale University Press, 2012.

Merton, Thomas. *The Inner Experience: Note on Contemplation*. New York: Harper, 2003.

Milne, Alan Alexander. *The Pooh Story Book*. London: Dutton, 1965.

Moore, Gareth. *A Question of Truth*. New York: Continuum, 2003.

Nolasco, Rolf. *Compassionate Presence: A Radical Response to Human Suffering*. Eugene, OR: Cascade, 2016.

———. *The Contemplative Counselor: A Way of Being*. Minnesota: Fortress, 2011.

Ogden, Pat, and Janina Fisher. *Sensorimotor Psychotherapy: Interventions for Trauma and Attachment*. New York: Norton, 2014.

Paris, Jenell Williams. *The End of Sexual Identity: Why Sex is Too Important to Define Who We Are*. Westmont: InterVarsity, 2011.

Pfaff, Donald W. *The Altruistic Brain: How We are Naturally Good*. Oxford: Oxford University Press, 2015.

Pierce, Brian J. *We Walk the Path Together: Learning from Thich Nhat Hanh and Meister Eckhart*. Maryknoll: Orbis, 2005.

Rizzolatti, Giacomo, and Laila Craighero. "The Mirror-Neuron System." *Annual Review of Neuroscience* 27 (2004) 169–92.

Rabe, André. *Desire Found Me: Exploring the Unconscious Movements of Desire—How They Form Us, Connect Us, Shape Our Greatest Ideas, Mold Our Societies, Influence Human History, and Ultimately, How They Are Unveiled*. N.p.: Rabe, 2014. Kindle edition.

Rosenberg, Morris. *Society and the Adolescent Self-Image*. Princeton Legacy Library. Princeton: Princeton University Press, 1965.

Rothschild, Zachary K., et al. "A Dual-Motive Model of Scapegoating: Displacing Blame to Reduce Guilt or Increase Control." *Journal of Personality and Social Psychology* 102 (2012) 1148–63.

Scanzoni, Lethda Dawson, and Virginia Ramey Mollenkott. *Is the Homosexual My Neighbor? A Positive Christian Response*. New York: HarperSanFrancisco, 1994.

Schwagger, Raymund. *Must There be Scapegoats? Violence and Redemption in the Bible*. San Francisco: Harper & Row, 1987.

Sedgwick, Eve Kosofsky. *Epistemology of the Closet*. Los Angeles: University of California Press, 1990.

Siegel, Daniel. *The Mindful Brain*. New York: Norton, 2007.

Spargo, Tamsin. *Foucault and Queer Theory*. New York: Icon, 1999.

Sullivan, Nikki. *A Critical Introduction to Queer Theory*. New York: New York University Press, 2003.

Talvacchia, Kathleen, et al. *Queer Christianities: Lived Religion in Transgressive Forms*. New York: New York University Press, 2015.

Taylor, Kathleen. *Cruelty: Human Evil and the Human Brain*. Oxford: Oxford University Press, 2009.

Teehan, John. *In the Name of God: The Evolutionary Origins of Religious Ethics and Violence*. Oxford: Wiley-Blackwell, 2010.

Tolle, Eckhart. *A New Earth: Awakening to Your Life's Purpose*. New York: Penguin, 2006.

United Methodist Hymnal. Nashville: Abingdon, 1989.

Vasey-Suanders, Mark. *The Scandals of Evangelicals and Homosexuality, English Evangelical Texts, 1960–2010*. Surrey: Ashgate, 2015.

Vines, Matthew. *God and the Gay Christian: The Biblical Case in Support of Same-Sex Relationships*. New York: Convergent, 2015.

Vittorio, Gallese, et al. "Action Recognition in the Premotor Cortex." *Brain* 119 (1996) 593–609.

Volf, Miroslav. "Human Flourishing." In *Renewing the Evangelical Mission*, edited by Richard Lints, 13–30. Grand Rapids: Eerdmans, 2013.

WCCM. "One in Christ with James Alison & Sarah Bachelard." https://soundcloud.com/wccm/one-in-christ-james-alison-sarah-bachelard-150518/s-q2Rkr.

Weedon, Christ. *Feminist Practice and Poststructuralist Theory*. Chicago: Wiley-Blackwell, 1987.

"What is Mimetic Theory?" https://violenceandreligion.com/mimetic-theory/.

Williams, James. *The Girard Reader*. New York: Crossroad, 1976.

Wilson, Ken, et al. *A Letter to my Congregation: An Evangelical Pastor's Path to Embracing People Who Are Gay, Lesbian, Bisexual, and Transgender into the Company of Jesus*. Canton: Spirit Books, 2014.

Wink, Walter. *Engaging the Powers*. Minneapolis: Fortress, 1992.

Index

Made in United States
North Haven, CT
05 October 2022

25047411R00078